Praise for Pirate Money

Do you know the basis for the valuation of money? Do you understand the impact of rapidly escalating interest rates and inflation on your financial well-being? Do you know how to protect your financial privacy and how to avoid being canceled for political reasons? Do you understand the future of digital currency? Do you know how excess national debt is likely to result in a financial crisis that will usher in a need for a new financial system? This book, *Pirate Money*, provides answers for all of these perplexing issues, but more importantly, provides some insights for those who want to participate in the protection of their financial future.

–**Dr. Ben Carson**, Chairman and Founder, the American Cornerstone Institute and 17th United States Secretary of Housing and Urban Development

Kevin Freeman has written a surprising, readable, and important book, which explains to a layperson just how dangerous CBDCs are - the digital currencies heading for us like freight trains - and reveals innovative solutions such as returning in modern ways to the ancient precious metals. Along the way we get fascinating explanations of 18th-century currencies, the intentions of the Founders regarding economics, what really causes inflation, and how you can protect your assets in the maelstrom ahead. Clear, original, and refreshing.

–**Dr. Naomi Wolfe**, CEO of DailyClout.io,
Bestselling Nonfiction Writer, Columnist

Kevin consistently unveils the underlying influences that intend to hold this country and its people financially hostage by his artful weaving of history and a commonsense approach.

–**Dick Uihlein**, CEO Uline

Kevin is a patriot and his new book, *Pirate Money*, is a great tool to learn about our financial system and the money that powers it.

–**Andrew Hughes,** Executive Director and CEO,
American Cornerstone Institute

It is amazing to observe how the very concept of "money" is changing right before our eyes these days. The implications for society, commerce, and even freedom are profound. Freeman, in *Pirate Money,* does a wonderful job enlightening readers to the opportunities and risks these changes present. Even better, he provides a map that we all can follow to protect what matters most and flourish in these unchartered waters.

–**Dr. Erik Davidson**, CFA, CTFA, Assistant Clinical Professor of Finance, Baylor University and Retired Chief Investment Officer of Wells Fargo Private Bank

It was God who granted private property rights to His people whom He had miraculously rescued from slavery in Egypt. God expected his people to work hard, provide for their own families, be compassionate to those with genuine need and to be honest in business. The use of "unjust weights and measures" – whether by a dishonest businessman or a dishonest king - was called an abomination. Inflation caused by expanding the money supply with fiat currency has always been a tool of despotism. While corrupt governments expand their power by inflating their own supply of money, the existing money saved by the people loses value leading to their poverty and total dependence on the government. Sound money is a safeguard to the people and demands responsibility from the people's government. We are experiencing the devastating effects of inflation in America today with the poorest among us suffering the most. Kevin Freeman not only identifies the problem in *Pirate Money*, but also provides real solutions.

–**Pastor Paul Blair,** Founder, Liberty Pastors Network & Training Camps

Imagine you go to the store tomorrow to buy a pound of hamburger and the butcher gives you a thimble of meat. Or you buy a "3,000 square foot house" that fits in the back of your pickup. The U.S. Constitution in Art. I, Sec. 8, cl. 4, empowers Congress to "fix the Standard of Weights and Measures" including "to coin Money, [and] regulate the Value thereof." In this masterful, must-read work by Kevin Freeman, you will see how a "Dollar" today is an untethered fraction of what the Founders intended, why it matters to us all, and what we can do about it.

–**The Honorable Ken Ivory**, Utah State Representative, Author of
Where's the Line? How States Protect the Constitution

In our season of severe economic uncertainty, I have learned to listen to Kevin Freeman. I first began following his speaking and writing 15 or more years ago. He was way ahead of his time then, and he is still ahead of the curve now. It is imperative, for your own financial security, that you study his writings. I have repeatedly interviewed Kevin Freeman and have learned so much every time. I take copious notes. Succinctly put, when Kevin speaks, listen. When Kevin writes, read it. You won't regret it if you do. In contrast, you will regret it if you don't. Read *Pirate Money.*

–**Dr. Jim Garlow**, CEO, Well Versed

Kevin Freeman's fascinating-to-read book, *Pirate Money,* covers all aspects of our money and paints a vivid picture of a sober reality: unless we act now to prevent it, the future of our money will not be about preserving our wealth or our freedoms. From old-fashioned inflation to central bank digital currencies (they call it "programable money") the administrative state elites want money to be an instrument of control. It's already happening in China with their linking digital money to their surveillance state social credit system. Unlike others who simply wring their hands, Kevin comes up with solutions and his proposal for a Texas-style gold-backed currency is something we should be looking hard at. All fiat money systems eventually collapse. Kevin's "gold bullet" may be what could save our money…and our liberty.

–**William L Walton**, Host, *The Bill Walton Show*,
Chairman, Resolute Protector Foundation

Kevin Freeman is not only one of America's preeminent experts in economic warfare. He is one of our most creative practitioners in this battlespace. This extraordinarily timely book is an indispensable how-to manual designed to equip freedom-loving Americans and states to defeat enemies, foreign and domestic, determined to use Central Bank Digital Currencies and similar "global governance" gambits to achieve world hegemony. Read *Pirate Money* and fight back now!

–**Frank Gaffney**, Executive Chairman, Center for Security Policy,
Host of *Securing America*

A must read from one of America's top experts in economic warfare. The once over-the-horizon financial threats that Kevin Freeman warned Pentagon leaders of decades ago are now fully upon us. As the U.S. today wages ad hoc economic war abroad and Americans endure financial assault here at home, what we really need is a plan. *Pirate Money* offers just this.

Freeman frames the fight we now face and offers a bold potential strategy by searching in one of Washington, D.C.'s least known places: the Constitution. There, carefully reserved by our Founders, lies a possible route to defeat the enemy, while saving us from ourselves.

–**Thomas Emanuel Dans**, CFA, former Trump Administration - Counselor to
the Under Secretary for International Affairs, U.S. Treasury

As always Kevin is ahead of the times on an emerging economic issue. I found *Pirate Money* to be an incredibly interesting book that quickly lays out what, why, and how we must respond to the world's quickly changing monetary policies. Americans have freedom and we need to use it quickly.

–**Cindi Castilla**, President, Texas Eagle Forum

I enjoyed this book, *Pirate Money*, as much as I enjoy talking with Kevin Freeman. Every time I do, I learn. Kevin has the ability to make complicated matters of financial affairs simple. He paints a picture of the challenges the American economy has experienced throughout our history. Using stories such as the "Wizard of Oz" and "Flipping the Monopoly Board," he parallels how our economic policy affects the everyday lives of people. Many have been dumbed down in their economic understanding of how money works. Kevin brings a real and practical path forward that has been with us since the beginning of time, all with the modern ease and convenience we know today as we transact business. NOW is the time to put action behind these words.

–**The Honorable Mark Dorazio**, Texas State Representative who sponsored Transactional Gold and Silver legislation

Pirate Money is truly worth its weight in Gold! Kevin Freeman provides us a glimpse into the past, an in-depth analysis of our present financial crisis, but most importantly a Constitutional, Biblical, and realistic solution for the future that can protect our money and our Republic from the impending collapse of the US dollar, and from the global plan to implement a government-backed CBDC. The first will destroy us financially and the second will enslave us permanently by controlling every aspect of our lives. *Pirate Money* needs to be read, shared, and actions taken by every American, NOW, before it's too late!

–**Ron Armstrong**, President, Stand Up Michigan

After serving in the House and Senate for 14 years, I am certain that Congress will continue to spend, borrow, and expand our debt; and the Federal Reserve will continue to print money to buy our debt until they bankrupt the country and destroy the value of the dollar. States must act now to create gold- and silver-backed currency. This will not only protect their citizens but eventually force the federal government to do the same. Kevin Freeman's *Pirate Money* is the playbook states need to accomplish this goal.

–**The Honorable Jim DeMint**, Former United States Senator

A dangerous precedent in the modern American culture, is one of total neglect of fiscal responsibility. Hanging in the balance is the security of our nation and our ability to maintain the leading position for good in the world. The path that Kevin is charting speaks to practical solutions for our nation at a critical time.

–**Jaco Booyens,** Abolitionist, anti-human trafficking, author, speaker, film director and lover of Jesus

In the Bible, we are told that those who do evil love the darkness. I thank God for Kevin Freeman's courage and willingness to shine a righteous light on Biden's managed decline of the USA and China's steps to push our country off the fiscal cliff. Pirate Money has answers for our nation and your money.

–**The Honorable Ken Blackwell**, Former State Treasurer of Ohio

Once you grasp that economic and monetary policy is almost entirely about the future of your freedom and not about money, that there are nefarious forces hard at work in this world determined to take away everyone's economic freedom and they are on the verge of success, and that the simple, constitutional, brilliant, pragmatic, solution spelled out in this book is available for everyone, you will know you should read *Pirate Money*, and pass it along to everyone you know. This solution is not about returning the dollar to the gold standard, it's about enabling everyone to use gold as currency. It's about freedom. Kevin Freeman is an invaluable 'American patriot expert'--and he's delivered an urgent Paul Revere-like warning of what is coming down the financial pike, and a thoroughly sound solution that every state can implement to protect its citizens and ultimately our sovereign, independent America.

–**Debbie Georgatos**, Host, *America, Can We Talk?*

Kevin Freeman's newest book, *Pirate Money*, is a map to a hidden treasure of Liberty, Security, and Values. Want economic freedom and Justice? This book has the answer. NO to CBDC and programmable money! YES to state-based transactional gold and silver with privacy and security. Easy to read, easy to understand, I highly recommend this book!

–**Charlie Kirk**, Founder and CEO, Turning Point USA, Host, *The Charlie Kirk Show*

Best-selling author Freeman has hit another home run with this thoroughly researched, immensely educative, and solution-oriented book! It is, "All You Ever Wanted to Know About Inflation, U.S. Debt, CBDCs, World Economic Forum, Our Dollar as a Reserve Currency, but Did Not Know Enough to Ask." Our financial security has been pirated by the elitist Captains and the Kings, but Freeman explains how we can take over the pirate's ship, steer it ourselves and use *Pirate Money* to put the elitists on the plank meant for us.

–**The Honorable Allen B. Clark**, Author of *Soldiers Blood and Bloodied Money: Wars and the Ruling Elites*

Pirate Money is a must-read book dealing with one of the most important threats facing our nation, and more importantly, offering solutions that could save our country. Kevin has created a masterpiece. I can't recommend the book highly enough.

–**Alex Newman**, Journalist/Author/Educator exposing evil

Kevin Freeman has done it again! His unwavering commitment to exposing evil and the evil agenda is a blessing to those that take time to read and educate themselves in this spiritual war. Kudos to Kevin and his faithful life companion, Marnie, who has been by his side unwaveringly as they attempt to expose the dark side. I have constantly told people that this guy knows stuff – and, once again, he has proven me right! Buy *Pirate Money*, read it, and pass it on. The easiest way to lose this war is to remain uneducated and uninvolved. Thank God for the Freemans!

–**Art Ally**, President, Timothy Partners, Ltd., Sponsors of The Timothy Plan

I know Kevin Freeman. I am convinced Kevin has a Silver Bullet strategy from God for the coming World Economic Crisis. God solutions for man-made problems. We are not helpless or hopeless. God is faithful and always will be. Be encouraged. Read *Pirate Money*!

–**Richard Bartlett MD**, Discoverer of The Silver Bullet protocol for COVID,
Recipient of The HHS Meritorious Service Award

This short read is exactly the antidote to corporate greed and government overreach. Don't say you weren't warned.

–**Kevin Sorbo**, Award-winning filmmaker

Kevin Freeman has a unique eye on macro-economic forces and how they can be used for good and evil. In *Pirate Money*, he lays out precisely how our enemies wish us evil (and can achieve their aims), and how we can with a couple of key moves enable our country and its citizens to defend and realize financial liberty and freedom.

–**James Dickey**, CEO, JD Key Consulting

The rolling out of Central Bank Digital Currencies, combined with national digital IDs, will form a digital gulag -- the foundation of the Great Reset. No one has done more to sound the alarm about CBDCs and to propose a workable, Constitutional solution than Kevin Freeman -- a brilliant economic analyst and force of nature.

–**Reggie Littlejohn**, President, Women's Rights Without Frontiers,
co-founder, Sovereignty Coalition

EVERYONE inherently knows something is up with their money…they KNOW that inflation hits them hard…they likely just don't know the facts Kevin lays out so well in *Pirate Money*. I can't imagine that 1 in 1,000 Americans know that what costs $1 today could be bought for 12 ½ cents in 1971! You owe it to yourself and those you lead to read this book, get educated and help others understand a piece of what Kevin Freeman has spent his career studying and learning about.

If you follow *Economic War Room*, you've gotten a taste, but for the facts laid out in an easy-to-read brief format, you need to read this book now! The Founders gave us a Republic, and Benjamin Franklin actually told a lady, "If you can keep it." That part depends on us and our willingness to know what has made our nation so special so that we know what we must do to preserve us a nation! Thank you, Kevin!

–**Chad Connelly**, Founder and CEO, Faith Wins

Kevin Freeman is one of those individuals who doesn't mind challenging the status quo! He pushes headlong into some of the gravest concerns of our day with the determination to find better solutions through Godly principles and his vast knowledge base in both national security and financial issues! He takes readers of *Pirate Money* along this journey with him and does so in a way that keeps the everyday patriot engaged and equipped to not just read a book but be moved to action!

–**Trayce Bradford**, Eagle Forum National Issue Chair on Human Trafficking; Former President, Texas Eagle Forum

Pirate Money by Kevin Freeman is an enlightening revelation, uncovering the hidden economic warfare that threatens our Nation's freedom. It is more than a book; it is an essential tool for preserving the principles our Founding Fathers fought for.

–**The Honorable Tan Parker**, Texas State Senator

Kevin Freeman is a brilliant and courageous leader. His *Economic War Room* financial insights are urgently needed to understand what is happening in the world today! I encourage every American to be armed with the wisdom of Kevin Freeman's new book *Pirate Money*!

–**William J. Federer**, best-selling author, and nationally known speaker

If federalism encourages experimentation, then Freeman gives a compelling argument that Texas is ripe for the most impactful economic experiment ever conceived in the area of central banking. He clearly maps out how Texas law, the US Constitution and various Supreme Court Decisions allow a clear alternative to CBDCs. No macroeconomist worth their salt should pass on Freeman's idea given the massive potential upside. *Pirate Money* is a must-read for anyone who values empirics over blind faith, especially in the field of monetary policy.

–**Philip M. Parker PhD** (Wharton), INSEAD Chair Professor of Management Science

Finances and freedom are intertwined, and this book, *Pirate Money*, is the key to unlocking your virtual handcuffs.

–**Sam Sorbo**, Best-selling author of *Words for Warriors*

Kevin Freeman's new book, *Pirate Money*, is a force for good and everyone should read it and quickly pass it along to others. Freeman explains the positive solution, embraced by America's founders, for combatting the evil of politicians who indenture the people they're called to serve, with debt that can never be repaid. There is hope and a way out of national indebtedness—but we need to get a critical mass of people "up to speed" on this practical, doable solution. I'm on board with *Pirate Money*, and I know you'll be, too!

–**The Honorable Michele Bachmann**, Former US Representative; Dean, Robertson School of Government, Regent University

Understanding money is the key to freedom. *Pirate Money* is a must-read for anybody who wants to fight for freedom.

–**Steve Kwast**, Lieutenant General (Ret) US Air Force; CEO, Skycorp Inc.

The dollar has lost 87% of its value since Nixon closed the gold window. Kevin Freeman shows how we can stop the bleeding, quickly, once and for all.

–**Rod D. Martin**, J.D., Founder and CEO The Martin Organization, Inc.

Economic warfare expert Kevin Freeman succinctly outlines the looming threats to our finances and freedom - both foreign and domestic - and he provides a biblical, Constitutional, and common-sense solution for "we the people" and our state governments to address those threats. *Pirate Money* is not only a "must-read" for freedom-loving Americans and their elected officials, but also a path to preserving that freedom.

–**Lt. Col. Tommy Waller**, USMC (Ret.), President & CEO, Center for Security Policy

Even as a finance major, I hated economics in school for the same reason I hated history...boring teachers and teaching methods. Kevin Freeman radically changes that by making this vitally important subject interesting and making it applicable to our lives. And yes, he even makes it entertaining and fun. Most importantly, the timing is critical and the blueprint he provides gives us hope for restoring fiscal sanity to the greatest nation in the history of mankind.

–**Rick Green**, America's Constitution Coach & Founder of Patriot Academy

It is wrong to call good evil and evil good. I am reminded that the principle of separation of economy and political direction necessarily dictates the preservation of sound money as an inalienable right of free men. A sovereign individual or society by definition is free of bondage found in unsound money. Bondage, being the absence of liberty is as evil as unsound money. This book shows a path back to sound money!

–**J. Christopher Byrd**, Esq. CPA, MBA

I found *Pirate Money* so good that I stopped very quickly and did something that I had never done before. I had my 20-year-old assistant read it out loud to me, so I could just concentrate on what was written. This was a first time for me. The information was so powerful. Part of the reason was the clarity, energy, how compelling the writing was that we did not want to stop reading. The book has a warmth and a personal feeling with the reader that was conveyed so well. My assistant said that for something that is applicable today and tomorrow, it is the best book he has read.

–**Somers White**, CPAE, FIMC, Management Consultant with
Important Company Clients on Six Continents

The US Constitution allows states to coin gold and silver as legal tender. Kevin Freeman's book *Pirate Money* explains how this could greatly benefit the hard-working people of America.

–**Scott O'Grady**, Veteran; best-selling author

Every person in America should read this book! This is a critical time in the history of our nation and Kevin Freeman is throwing out an economic life-line that could help save the US while there is still time. I highly recommend it. This plan offers "a financial ark" to save the money of believers.

–**Dr. Cindy Jacobs**, prophet, speaker, teacher, and author

Kevin Freeman's *Pirate Money* is a must-read for anyone who is interested in potential solutions to America's monetary crisis. If Joe Biden and Davos elites have it their way, the value of the dollar will continue to plummet. Even worse, your privacy and freedom could soon disappear because of the rise of central bank digital currencies, another power-grab supported by the Biden administration. We need real answers to those problems, and Freeman's *Pirate Money* could prove to be an important source for those answers, as well as an excellent first step on the road to saving the United States.

–**Justin Haskins**, Director, Socialism Research Center,
The Heartland Institute

PIRATE MONEY

Discovering the Founders' Hidden Plan for Economic Justice and Defeating the Great Reset

KEVIN D. FREEMAN

LibertyHawk Publishing is an imprint of EWR-Media Holdings, LLC.

Pirate Money: Discovering the Founders' Hidden Plan for Economic Justice and Defeating the Great Reset

Cover Art and Interior Design: Russell Lake
Photos: Jason Shane

ISBN: 978-1-958945-04-9 (Paperback Edition)

ISBN: 978-1-958945-05-6 (Hardcover Edition)

ISBN: 978-1-958945-06-3 (Kindle Edition)

Library of Congress Control Number (LCCN): 2023944384

Published by LibertyHawk Publishing.

Printed in the United States of America.

First Edition.
2 3 4 5 6 7 8 9 10

PIRATE MONEY

Discovering the Founders' Hidden Plan for Economic Justice and Defeating the Great Reset

KEVIN D. FREEMAN

LibertyHawk Publishing • Argyle, Texas

This book is dedicated to the Creator of Life,
the Author of Truth, the One
who demands honest weights and measures.

If you aren't faithful with your unrighteous mammon,you will never be trusted with true wealth.

—Jesus (Luke 16:11, paraphrased)

CONTENTS

Nick with Kevin on the set of
Economic War Room.

FOREWORD

by Nick Vujicic

When I first visited LibertyHawk Ranch I had no idea what to expect. The property name was certainly intriguing. And I'd heard of Kevin Freeman from his BlazeTV show, *Economic War Room with Kevin Freeman*. But who was he? Economists are stuffy and more often than not, terribly wrong. Worse than weather forecasters. When you get things wrong about money, people get hurt. And they never seem to have answers. Only problems. Economics is known as "the dismal science." Dismal for sure, but science? Hardly! To make it worse, I was visiting what in effect was a "dismal science" war room. Could it get more depressing?

I'm always living on the bright side. As a man born without limbs, I'm forced to deal with daily challenges that most everyone else takes for granted. Thus, I rely on Christ for a spirit of gratitude and a "can do" attitude. My trip to LibertyHawk, however, was a little more somber. I knew we were in an Economic War because I had recently had my bank account closed without explanation. To this day, I don't understand why. I'm no terrorist. I pay my bills on time. I'm actually a great customer. But inexplicably, the bank no longer wanted my business. Shortly after that, I accepted my friend Betsy Gray's offer to explore establishing a proposed Pro-Life Bank where customers would be welcomed rather than kicked out.

I guess that sort of sounded like an Economic War thing, so my friend Jim Garlow connected me with Kevin. A week or so later, Betsy and I were at LibertyHawk Ranch. It was nothing like I had imagined. Yes, the *Economic War Room*® was there. Kevin's beautiful wife Marnie greeted us, and we sensed the place was anointed. There's a powerful spirit of prayer over the property and all the people are amazing, Mike, Russell, and Van. Marnie gave us a tour of the Dunkirk Advance Center. We visited the lodges. We worshipped at the prayer garden. Only then did we have a meeting.

Rather than a robotic economist focused only on charts and graphs, I found Kevin to be truly human and a fervent believer in Christ. Warm, funny, and engaging. And smart. Don't get me wrong. He has all the credentials and diplomas, a CFA designation, 40 years in the investment field, and more than a decade as America's preeminent economic warfare expert. But what I found most intriguing was that Kevin had the same mindset as me. Rather than focusing on problems, he pursued solutions. If people were losing bank accounts because of political or religious beliefs, we need to build a bank that wouldn't do that. When a person is kicked out of their bank, they are essentially dehumanized, and Kevin understood. More than that, he jumped in to help solve the problem.

I share all of this because it's not just Nick Vujicic who had banking cancelled. It is also Sam Brownback, a former U.S. Senator and Ambassador. It is also Nigel Farage in London who led the BREXIT movement. If they can do it to us, they will do it to you if you step out of line. It's only a matter of time. This is 21st century control. With advancing technology, it will only get worse. This is Economic Warfare, and we need solutions. Kevin Freeman is our man for such a time as this.

Pirate Money explains the threats. These include inflation, massive government debt, CBDC, targeted debanking, the World Economic Forum, the dollar's precarious status as reserve currency, and Chinese Unrestricted Warfare. More importantly, however, it offers a profound solution. One that was hidden in the Constitution more than 200 years ago. One that will work today if we can find the political will to implement it. It's not a hard task. It is an essential one.

I challenge you to read *Pirate Money* and share it with everyone you know. This isn't only for those on the political left or right. It isn't just for Republicans or Democrats. It's not just for the wealthy or the poor. This is about Economic Justice and reading it will make a real difference in your everyday life. Don't be intimidated. The story is readable, personal, and compelling. You will understand it and more importantly gain clarity on what must be done to make things right again.

As the book explains, we have been playing the game Monopoly, using Monopoly money, with a banker who cheats. The money system should be fair. It's what God's word demands. But for too long that hasn't been the case. It's time for that to change. This book shows us how in a very accessible manner.

I am reminded of Isaiah 33 which starts with a statement about those who are plundering and dealing treacherously. Sounds a lot like what we are facing now. But then, the prophet cries out to God. In verse 6, we see the hope and solution:

> "Wisdom and knowledge will be the stability of your times,
> *And* the strength of salvation;
> The fear of the Lord *is* His treasure."
> -Isaiah 33:6 (NKJV)

Our solution is thus threefold:

1) *Acquire wisdom and knowledge,*
2) *Demonstrate stability and strength, and*
3) *Make the fear of the Lord our ultimate Treasure.*

This book is a treasure map. Let's follow it together.

Nick Vujicic
Servant of the Most-High God

Pirate Money

INTRODUCTION

Why Pirates?

When I first started writing this book, I knew that "pirate" would be in the title. The book is about money, the wealth gap, the Great Reset, Central Bank Digital Currency, and Chinese efforts to displace the American dollar. More importantly, though, it is about implementing a solution to provide Economic Justice for real people facing the severe challenges headed straight toward us all. And I believe that solution has a pirate element in it. When you finish reading, I think you'll agree. We are about to go on a *National-Treasure*-style hunt, searching through clues left by the Founders of this great Republic. They lived in a world of pirates. To learn their hidden secret, we'll have to change our thinking. This book is a map to that treasure.

It's About MONEY

Many things in life are primarily determined by our perspective. Money included.

For example, were you aware that the purchasing power of the dollar bills in your wallet has declined 87% (according to official government inflation measures) since 1971?[1,2] Basically, everything costs about eight times as much now as it did back then. Wow! How did that happen?

In 1971, President Nixon shocked the world by abandoning the gold standard.[3] He said it was "temporary."[4] The move made international waves but has been largely forgotten.

But is it true that what costs $1 today could be bought for 12 ½ cents in 1971?

That's factual, for sure, based on official government inflation statistics (which are likely understated by a lot). The Federal Reserve notes you have in your wallet certainly buy a lot less today than they did 50 years ago. I remember that you could once buy a good candy bar for a dime. Now, it costs upwards of $2. Every American has felt the very real pinch of inflation.

Let's be honest, though. You may not even have paper bills in your wallet. Everything is digital and you probably use debit and credit cards. Even those are antiquated compared to ApplePay, AliPay, and Google Pay. Still, all of this is based on the dollar unit which is at its core unbacked "fiat" money.[5] Fiat comes from Latin and can be translated as "so let it be." This means that if the government says it is worth something, it is.[6] It is not backed by any physical commodity, just how much you trust the government.

1. https://blogs.cfainstitute.org/investor/2013/03/13/president-nixon-the-man-who-sold-the-world-fiat-money/
2. https://www.in2013dollars.com/us/inflation/1971
3. https://financialpost.com/fp-finance/how-richard-nixon-rocked-the-world-50-years-ago-with-just-the-greenback-and-gold
4. https://www.imf.org/external/about/histend.htm
5. https://www.investopedia.com/terms/f/fiatmoney.asp
6. https://en.wiktionary.org/wiki/fiat

Regardless of how you carry money, one thing is for certain. American dollars have lost purchasing power regardless of the time period you consider. Since 2000, inflation has made things 76% more expensive.[7] Even since 2020, prices have gone up nearly 20%.[8]

But here is another perspective. Maybe the dollar has not lost value over 50 years.

What???? How Can That Be?

It depends on how you define the term. The word "dollar" as used by the Founders of the United States (and the authors of the Constitution) referred to something much more specific than a dirty green piece of paper with the picture of a dead President. It referred to a silver coin issued by Spain, a "Spanish milled dollar," to be precise.[9] The value of this dollar was defined by weight and purity of silver in an amount well understood by the public through commercial transactions. This is explained by Edwin Vieira in a November 1994, article published by the Foundation for Economic Education (FEE), titled, "*What is a Dollar?*"

> *History shows that the real "dollar" is a coin containing 371.25 grains (troy) of fine silver. Both Article I, Section 9, Clause 1 of the Constitution, and the Seventh Amendment use the noun "dollar." The Constitution does not define the "dollar," though, because in the late 1700s everyone knew that the word meant the silver Spanish milled dollar. The Founding Fathers did not need explicitly to adopt the "dollar" as the national unit of money or to define the "dollar" in the Constitution, because the Continental Congress had already done so.*

7. https://www.in2013dollars.com/us/inflation/2000?amount=100
8. https://www.in2013dollars.com/us/inflation/2020?amount=100
9. https://fee.org/articles/what-is-a-dollar/

The American Colonies did not originally adopt the dollar from England, but from Spain. Under that country's monetary reforms of 1497, the silver real (réal) became the Spanish money of account. A new coin consisting of eight reales also appeared. Known as pesos, duros, piezas de a ocho ("pieces of eight"), or Spanish dollars, the coins achieved predominance in the New World because of Spain's then-important commercial and political position.[10]

That's sort of cool. **The original concept of dollar was based on a "piece of eight," which we know best as pirate treasure!**[11]

What made it a "piece of eight" was the contents of 371.25 grains (troy) of fine silver. That is 0.7734 troy ounces of fine silver (a troy ounce is 480 grains). You could divide that dollar into eight pie-shaped wedges, each valued at 12.5 cents. Two bits make a quarter, and four quarters make a dollar.

When you look at the purchasing power of the silver in a "piece of eight" over the past 50 years, you would have actually gained ground relative to the price of goods and services. From this perspective, a "dollar" has more than held its value.

A good example can be seen in the price of gasoline. Did you know that people used to buy five gallons for a dollar (or ten dimes) a hundred years ago? Would you be surprised if I told you that the

10. Ibid
11. https://www.bbc.co.uk/ahistoryoftheworld/objects/WBNKU2ssSQuBVLGmNX5UAg

same deal is available today?[12] That's true if you pay for the gas using the metal value of pre-1964 (90% silver) dimes (worth more than $20).[13] Every once in a while, a filling station will offer a gallon of gas for a (silver) dime or two just to prove the point.[14,15]

The wealthy have the means to not only overcome inflation but also to profit from it. That was true in 1776 and remains true today. But contrary to what they try to pass off as history today, America was founded for "We the People," not just the elite. It's time to reorient our thinking and learn the Founder's hidden plan for Economic Justice. They fought, sacrificed, and even died for you to have it.[16] Don't let it be stolen now. It starts with a dollar.

Are dollars good or bad? Depends on what you call a dollar.

This book will hopefully broaden your perspective on money, identify threats facing you, and show you a way to protect yourself and your family. Beyond that, you will learn how money can and should be freedom.

Over the past 50 years, inflation has been the biggest threat to your money. But it will seem like a minor annoyance compared to what's coming. Threats have emerged both inside and outside our nation that could soon make your own money your worst enemy.

This raises the key question, borrowing a phrase from Capital One. "What's in your wallet?"

You are about to find out. And it's likely not good. But it can be. Let's learn how.

12. https://www.bullionvault.com/gold-news/silver_price_gas_prices_080220115
13. https://sdbullion.com/blog/how-much-silver-in-a-silver-dime
14. https://www.nytimes.com/1979/10/14/archives/gas-at-10c-a-gallon-if-paid-in-silver-coins.html
15. https://www.washingtonpost.com/archive/local/1980/01/22/gasoline-at-10-cents-a-gallon-only-if-smitty-likes-your-silver/48b61088-e27c-4f93-bee7-4d8f2dbcf179/
16. https://www.jfklibrary.org/archives/other-resources/john-f-kennedy-speeches/charleston-sc-19420704

Here be treasure, matey.
—unknown pirate

1

WHAT MONEY SHOULD BE

What is the Future of Money?

There is a lot of talk regarding new forms of money like bitcoin, Central Bank Digital Currency (CBDC), and all-electronic funds that will soon eliminate cash.[17] We already have "tap to pay" with your watch or smart phone. But what's coming will go further, where everything is digital, start to finish. With convenience come concerns of privacy and control. What happens if your money is hacked, tracked, or worse yet, turned off? Or, what if you forget the passcode to your digital wallet? Certainly, there are pluses and minuses with these modern attempts at currency and we will explore them.

Paper money has its problems as well, inflation being chief among them. Dirty green pieces of paper also can be inconvenient to carry and lots of places have stopped accepting cash. The former mayor of

17. https://www.kitco.com/news/2023-05-31/The-future-of-banking-is-in-blockchain-and-AI-RBI-Governor-Jain.html

Chicago, Lori Lightfoot, told residents to stop carrying cash unless they wanted to be mugged.[18] Besides that, your wallet can only hold so many bills. Would you really want to lug wheelbarrows of paper money to pay your mortgage every month? Online bill pay is so much easier.

Checking accounts, debit cards, credit cards, and the modern banking system work pretty well. But you've probably noticed that, while more convenient than wads of cash, they, too, are impacted by inflation. The buying power of your checking and savings falls every time that prices go up. And then there are fees, overdraft charges, and a host of regulations with which to contend. Finally, there is the emerging threat of cancellation if you hold views "out of the mainstream," work in a disapproved area, or the bank simply doesn't like you.[19]

There are a lot of ways that modern money is better than money from the olden days like gold "doubloons" and silver "pieces of eight." It would be hard to lug around "pirate money" from the days of Captain Morgan, Long John Silver, and Blackbeard.[20] And who has time to bury that treasure on a remote desert island? And what if you lose the map, where "X" marks the spot? Overall, the attraction of pirate money, however, is not its convenience but the fact that it has proven to be a good store of value. Over time, gold and silver coins have maintained their purchasing power but are far from easy to get, hold, and spend.

Rather than starting with what is wrong about various forms of money, why not begin with an ideal and then see how best to achieve it?

18. https://katv.com/news/nation-world/chicago-mayor-tells-residents-to-stop-using-cash-if-they-dont-want-to-keep-getting-mugged-lori-lightfoot-digital-payment#
19. https://www.electionforum.org/christian-persecution/warning-to-christians-theyre-coming-for-you-says-rev-graham/
20. https://youtu.be/NxnDeooQGCo

WHAT MONEY SHOULD BE

Money is central to life in so many ways. Maybe too many, at least in America. But there is little doubt that you need money to live. Further, having money lets you do many wonderful things. Money can save lives by allowing good nutrition, clean water, housing, or proper medical care. Money can open doors through education or training. Money can support invention, fund creativity, access resources, and expand horizons. The key is the proper use of money. Sure, there are lots of downsides to money if taken or used the wrong way. But overall, it's better to have money (as long as it does not have you).

The question for most people is never really whether you want money. It really is, how do you want it? Each form of money has plusses and minuses. So how do we get the best of all worlds?

We are going to skip ahead of all the history, definitions, functions, risks, and pitfalls and get right to it. **What pirates used for money, made legal tender, guarded by the state, made transactional, and open to all people with privacy, convenience, and stability is what money should be.** We will show you why and how to get there!

Money is Freedom ... or at least it used to be

In and of itself, money is just a thing. Dirty green pieces of paper. Ones and zeros on a computer. Or shiny rocks. To me, as a 10-year-old kid, however, money meant freedom.

I remember what it was like to be 10 years old (even if it was more than half a century ago). If I had a dime, I had a Hershey's bar. Fifteen cents would entertain me with a Spider-Man comic book. A quarter meant a Slurpee and change. A dollar bill got me a cheeseburger, fries, and a chocolate shake. Those were the days. Money meant freedom and a summer of fun. I could earn $1.60 with one hour's work cutting the lawn, enough to buy everything I wanted.[21] But if I'd kept the cash for the past half century, it would barely buy just the candy bar today.

When I was young, we had "Five & Dime stores."[22] Everything cost a nickel or a dime. They were killed by the inflation of the 1970s. Today, there are dollar stores but now the cheapest stuff you can buy is $1.25.[23] The newer thing is Five Below, where you can get stuff for $5 that was once well under a dollar at the Five & Dime. Even there, prices are going up.[24]

KEVIN WITH COMIC AND SLURPEE BOUGHT IN THE 70S.

Money should be convenient, accessible, valuable, secure, useful, private, easy to acquire and easy to spend. It should hold its value over time. Be simple to calculate. And universally accepted. U.S. dollar bills were good enough in 1971 but no longer.

The ideal money today would be based in gold and silver, held and protected by a sovereign state, and available electronically. It's hard to properly pay for a cup of coffee with a one-ounce gold coin. What do you do? Shave off a thousandth of an ounce of gold and give Starbucks the dust? Then how do you know what you have left? But if that gold were in a Texas vault, for example, and the state

21. https://www.dol.gov/agencies/whd/minimum-wage/history#:~:text=The%20minimum%20wage%20went%20to,and%20%241.60%20in%20February%201971.
22. https://www.unitedstatesnow.org/what-is-a-five-and-dime.htm
23. https://thekrazycouponlady.com/tips/money/dollar-tree-raising-prices
24. https://www.news8000.com/lifestyle/money/five-below-starts-selling-products-for-more-than-5/article_a1bcf251-3c33-5db4-b37c-484d0a990a74.html

kept track down to minute fractions of an ounce of your holdings, and paid whomever you directed, it would be ideal money. A great store of value. A useful unit of account. And a powerful means of exchange.

Is such a system possible? It is! And it already exists, or at least a version of it does. What's more, I already use it.

Transactional Gold—almost perfect money?

There is a wonderful app on my iPhone that lets me keep money in the form of gold held in a Swiss vault. Once you open an account, you can add gold at any time and spend it at any time. It keeps track of everything. You can pay for stuff using gold with a MasterCard or simply by tapping your phone. It is safe, convenient, and accessible.

I got the Glint app just to test it out and it literally works great. I've bought gold twice and spent it twice. Easy to use. Almost seamless. And the restaurant where we dined had no idea they were paid in gold. To them it was just a credit card charge. I'd use it more often except for a couple of small drawbacks (not Glint's fault). Overall, the power it provides is amazingly impressive. Here is how Glint describes itself:

> *Glint believes in financial fairness for all. Glint was invented to liberate everyone from our current monetary system. For millennia, gold has been the trusted store of wealth. In today's world, it's a secure hedge against inflation and a stable currency when stock markets fluctuate. Glint offers an alternative to fiat currencies enabling our clients to buy, save, send, and spend allocated gold with the flexibility of Mastercard.*[25]

25. https://glintpay.com/us as accessed June 21, 2023.

This is very close to the vision I've espoused for more than a decade. It's simple, convenient, and affordable. You can hold money as gold and spend it as you need to. It becomes Transactional Gold, the Holy Grail of money.

The two small drawbacks? First, the gold is stored in Switzerland. Yes, it's in a Brinks Vault. And yes, it is insured by Lloyd's of London. But I was among the original supporters of the Texas Bullion Depository in Leander, Texas, and would prefer my gold to be held there.[26] The second concern I have is that because my Glint money is not officially "legal tender," it is subject to the taxation rules for gold, taxed as a commodity (in fact deemed a "collectible").[27] What that means is that if I buy gold via Glint (or any gold dealer) and the price of gold goes higher (which is the hope), I owe tax whenever I sell or spend it. What's worse, I'm required to report transactions to the IRS, meaning I lose some of the inflation protection and the privacy benefits I want.

Transactional Gold comes as close to a great monetary system as available in the world today. It works as an iPhone app! There are other gold-based debit cards (like Glint) available.[28] It's not backed by a government, but anyone who has studied history knows that private money has long been a part of our American experiment. Glint and gold-based debit offerings are just the most modern version of that illustrious heritage.

If I could wave a magic wand, I'd start with something like Glint and make it legal tender so it couldn't be taxed as a commodity. I'd add silver for multiple reasons. I'd promise privacy and back it by my home state, Texas. I'd hold a good part of my money there in gold and silver, pay for stuff with gold and silver, and never worry about bank runs or inflation.

26. https://www.texasbulliondepository.gov/
27. https://www.investopedia.com/articles/personal-finance/081616/understanding-taxes-physical-goldsilver-investments.asp
28. https://nomadcapitalist.com/finance/gold-backed-debit-card/

This isn't an entirely new concept. I've been thinking about it from the time I was a kid studying monetary theory, the Constitution, and, well pirates. OK, maybe I was a boring kid, apart from the pirates, comic books, and Slurpees. But I've always been fascinated with money and how it works. That led me into an investment career and eventually to the Pentagon as an Economic Warfare consultant.[29] In fact, I began to share with our Defense Department in 2008 that an Economic War was underway and the Phase Three of that war would be an all-out assault on the American dollar and our monetary system (and was the basis for my New York Times' bestseller, *Secret Weapon*).[30,31] My proposed solution? The same basic idea of pirate money (gold and silver) made modern and convenient (like Glint), but with the official authority of a state behind it (like Texas).

Over the summer of 2013 (published, January 2014), I wrote what would become an Amazon bestseller with the title, *Game Plan: How to Protect Yourself from the Coming Cyber-Economic Attack*.[32] In addition to action plans for individuals, I also outlined a national strategy to protect America. On page 223, I wrote:

> *Another initiative at the state level that merits attention is the Texas Bullion Depository, proposed by Representative Giovanni Capriglione with support from Governor Rick Perry and the approval of Jim Rickards, the*

29. https://www.washingtontimes.com/news/2011/feb/28/financial-terrorism-suspected-in-08-economic-crash/
30. https://www.thetrumpet.com/8047-economic-warfare-hastening-the-demise-of-america
31. https://www.regnery.com/9781596987944/secret-weapon/
32. https://www.amazon.com/Game-Plan-Protect-Yourself-Cyber-Economic/dp/1621572005/

> *author of Currency Wars. If the measure had passed, the state would have sold the billion dollars' worth of physical gold that it held in New York and bought an equivalent amount to be stored in Texas. The depository would be open to anyone seeking physical protection for his gold, making Texas an economic leader in the event of dollar catastrophe. There were even discussions about providing depositors with the equivalent of an ATM card, enabling them to exchange gold for goods, with electronic record keeping down to small fractions of an ounce.* ***With a Texas gold card, you could buy a pack of gum or cup of coffee with gold and never have to hold paper currency. Gold would be added to the seller's account or converted into dollars for exchange.*** *As long as the dollar held up, there would be no need to move to such a system. But in the case of a dollar failure, wouldn't it be good to have a contingency plan ready to go?*

Want to know the rest of the story? When first running for the Texas House, Giovanni Capriglione knocked on my door (early 2012).[33] I was already knee-deep in writing contingency plans for policymakers in case of a dollar failure. We sat on my porch for quite a while discussing monetary theory and the Constitution. The ideas I shared fit perfectly with his plan to move the gold owned by Texas from New York to our home state.[34] Opening a bullion depository became step #1 in a plan to create an alternative, state-based, Constitutional monetary system.[35] And you know what? Once elected, Representative Capriglione kept his promise! It took a couple of sessions, but the depository passed in 2015 and opened its doors in 2018.[36] Imagine that! A politician who kept his word!

33. https://votegiovanni.com/kevin-freeman-endorses-giovanni-capriglione/
34. https://schiffgold.com/key-gold-news/texas-gold-depository-could-challenge-federal-power/
35. https://www.theblaze.com/news/2015/10/19/how-texas-could-be-uniquely-prepared-if-the-u-s-dollar-collapses
36. https://www.bigcountryhomepage.com/news/main-news/texas-just-opened-the-nations-first-state-run-gold-depository-heres-what-that-means/

What we essentially have is a "proof of concept" with Glint and other gold-backed debit cards like it, combined with the infrastructure of a state-created depository system that could grant "legal tender" status, keep the gold (and silver) in Texas, and provide privacy protections as a matter of law. I've advocated this plan in hundreds of speeches and media appearances over the past decade.[37] And it has become one of the primary topics on our BlazeTV show, *Economic War Room with Kevin Freeman*.[38,39,40,41,42]

The goal is to take the bullion depository to the next level. As I explained in *Game Plan*, we want account holders to be able to use the equivalent of pirate money (gold doubloons and silver pieces of eight), hold it as legal tender, and spend it like cash with a debit card. We made a major push for the idea in the 88th Texas Legislature, even sponsoring a website to explain it.[43] There was an overwhelmingly positive response with a "take action" campaign generating over 2.8 million calls, letters, and emails in support![44]

---

37. https://www.theepochtimes.com/in-depth-texas-lawmakers-consider-creating-gold-based-digital-currency-for-use-by-anyone-anywhere_5267493.html
38. https://rumble.com/v2tqxmw-texas-transactional-gold-and-silver-update-and-plan-b-ep-247.html
39. https://rumble.com/v2kkpfq-monopoly-money-vs.-state-issued-gold-based-currency-guest-michael-maharrey-.html
40. https://xotv.me/channels/233-economic-war-room/vod_videos/15414-a-gold-bullet-for-central-bank-digital-currency-ep-224
41. https://xotv.me/channels/233-economic-war-room/vod_videos/14518-the-digital-texan-real-economic-justice-from-the-lone-star-state-guest-rod-martin-ep-192
42. https://xotv.me/channels/233-economic-war-room/vod_videos/14047-a-new-state-backed-gold-digital-currency-you-can-trust-ep-184
43. https://www.transactionalgold.com
44. https://alignact.com/go/texas-transactional-gold---next-steps---special-session

How it Works (as explained at TransactionalGold.com):

> "IMAGINE OPENING AN ACCOUNT, ENTERING YOUR BANK INFORMATION, AND CONVENIENTLY TRANSFERRING A PORTION OF YOUR MONEY INTO GOLD AND SILVER.
>
> Then when you go to a restaurant, use a TTC (Texas Transactional Currency) debit card to pay for your meal in gold, rather than paper money. It sounds like science fiction, but it is available today through commercial applications like Gold Debit Cards, but the gold is typically held in Switzerland.
>
> As Texans, our gold should be in Texas, and it comes with the other benefits being legal tender. If we put the existing Texas Bullion Depository together with existing commercial applications, you get gold- (or silver-) based, state-backed, constitutional money that works in a modern economy!
>
> It is NOT CBDC with all the possible privacy and control concerns. It is not at risk from attacks on the American dollar by Russia, China, the BRICS nations, or others.
>
> It is a place for everyday Americans to protect their finances!
>
> With these Texas bills, using gold every day is simple. It is just another way to pay! Every American, regardless of economic class, could have a portion of their assets held in gold as a protection against inflation, while still enjoying the same convenient access to their funds through use of a debit card."

Did We Win?

Unfortunately, despite valiant efforts, SB 2334 (filed by Senator Bryan Hughes and joint authored by Senator Tan Parker) and its companion HB 4903 (filed by Representative Mark Dorazio and joint authored by Representative Capriglione, Representative Raymond and three others with 37 co-authors) fell short of passage in a tumultuous legislative session. What we did win, however, was the hearts and minds of many Texans wanting a better type of money! Our bills went much further than anyone expected, setting the stage for round two, whether as a special session called by Governor Abbott, adoption by another state, or the 89th Texas Legislature convening in 2025.

THIS IS AN IDEA WHOSE TIME HAS COME!

Over the next few chapters, we will explain why this is so important and what we can do to make it happen. Unfortunately, the time is short. Enemies, both foreign and domestic, have targeted your wallets not just to take your money but also to strip your freedom.

Money is freedom ... or it should be. How do we get there?

I try all things; I achieve what I can.
—Herman Melville, *Moby-Dick*

2

THE FUTURE OF MONEY

At one time in America, money simply meant green paper with pictures of dead Presidents. Before that, it was coins with the image of rulers. Even 2,000 years ago, in the days of Jesus, money was a denarius coin bearing the image of Caesar.[45]

In the Internet Age, however, money is morphing into something entirely different. And the changes are not going to be good for you. Money, which has been freedom, will soon become slavery unless we act quickly. Shekels become shackles, to coin a phrase.

The Great Hope?

There's been huge excitement regarding bitcoin. From its inception as a white paper in 2008 (explaining the blockchain), bitcoin has captured imaginations around the world.[46] What is it? An investment?

45. https://www.biblegateway.com/passage/?search=Matthew%2022%3A18-22&version=NIV
46. https://money.usnews.com/investing/articles/the-history-of-bitcoin

Money? There's no doubt that it started a cryptocurrency revolution. Decentralized money giving power to the people! You have to love that!

At first, bitcoin was a novelty. A way to exchange value with privacy and convenience. Like PayPal 2.0 in a sense.[47] Bitcoin was launched in the aftermath of the 2008 financial crisis when the U.S. dollar was King, and our Federal Reserve was busy rescuing the world. Even the Chinese pegged their own currency to the dollar from 2008-10.[48] Bitcoin was an interesting way to use an emerging technology. Few imagined the monetary powerhouse it would become within a very short time.

The first commercial transaction occurred May 22, 2010, when Laszlo Hanyecz paid for two medium Papa John's pizzas with 10,000 bitcoins.[49] That shows what they were worth at the time, about 2/10ths of a penny each. When a single bitcoin reached $60,000 a couple of years ago, people made jokes about just how good those pizzas needed to be. In hindsight, they cost $30 million each! No wonder many people celebrate May 22 as "bitcoin pizza day."[50]

But is bitcoin money? It certainly functions like it and the technology has a great deal of promise. But there are many reasons why it is not and may never be money in the strictest sense and in its present form. First among them? The government hates bitcoin. They may not admit it, but it is true.

47. https://www.ebayinc.com/stories/news/paypal-remains-at-the-forefront-of-todays-digital-payments-revolution/
48. https://www.ft.com/content/72dbbe49-22b9-4154-8b37-afe19cfda0a2
49. https://www.coindesk.com/consensus-magazine/2023/05/22/celebrating-bitcoin-pizza-day-the-time-a-bitcoin-user-bought-2-pizzas-for-10000-btc/
50. https://nationaltoday.com/bitcoin-pizza-day/

What Makes Bitcoin Special?

There are really two powerful values to bitcoin beyond the way-cool blockchain. First, it is private and second, it is scarce. That may sound modest but is actually monumental. Privacy means that while everyone knows that a specific bitcoin exists, no one is certain to whom it belongs. Such anonymity is quite valuable, and not just to drug dealers and terrorists. No one wants their spending habits monitored and scrutinized. Privacy means freedom. You couldn't track the dime I used to buy a candy bar in 1970 or the dollar used for a cheeseburger, fries, and chocolate shake (even though every dollar bill has a serial number). There was never an easy way to know where our money had been or where it was going. That is until the digital age.

With credit cards and electronic checking, tracking money became instantaneous. That is one reason that bitcoin was so quickly adopted. All the convenience of digital but with the privacy of cash. HUGE!

The second value of bitcoin is the way it is designed. Bitcoin must be "mined," and that takes time. Mining the next bitcoin takes a little more effort than it did to produce the one before it. Mining is actually solving increasingly difficult mathematical equations with the reward being a new bitcoin given for the shared ledger. Mining also implies (as is the case here) that there are only so many bitcoins that will ever be produced, meaning that supply is limited.[51] There will only be 21 million coins ever available according to the design.[52] While technically bitcoin is a type of "fiat" money (not exchangeable for a commodity), the supply limit provides a basis for value.

This supply limitation is in sharp contrast to our American dollar, which seemingly has the printing presses running at full capacity

51. https://www.bankrate.com/investing/what-is-bitcoin-mining/
52. https://originstamp.com/blog/why-can-there-only-be-21-million-bitcoins

24/7.[53] Limited supply combined with great demand for this new type of money led to the massive spike in bitcoin price. From fractions of a penny to over $60,000 in about a decade (even though it fell after that peak). Bitcoin is a marvelous innovation and America should be leading the technology.

But is it money? I would argue that it has the theoretical potential to be money but is not now and might never be. I don't say that because I don't like bitcoin. I do. I say it because the government hates it.[54]

Aside from the volatility (which is a solvable problem), the two things that make bitcoin truly unique are the two things the government hates most about it. It is private and limited in supply. Governments don't want privacy because that means they can't track and control you. And they don't want limited supply in money. They love their printing presses. Even more, they love the ability to conjure digital money with ones and zeros.

Governments will feign support of bitcoin for a couple of reasons. They don't want to be seen as anti-innovation. They love the fortunes created by bitcoin and curry the favor of those who have them (like Sam Bankman Fried before he was exposed).[55] And they want the technology under their control. This is all so true that the whole notion of a government-backed cryptocurrency emerged.[56] We'll deal with that in a bit, but rest assured the way the Feds see it, it will not be a source of freedom.

The government has already begun its assault on bitcoin to soften the field and eliminate future competition to its own version soon to be released.[57] Theirs is a three-pronged assault:

53. https://www.usatoday.com/in-depth/money/2020/05/12/coronavirushow-u-s-printing-dollars-save-economy-during-crisis-fed/3038117001/
54. https://www.cnbc.com/2023/04/24/crypto-is-dead-in-america-says-tech-investor-chamath-palihapitiya.html
55. https://nypost.com/2022/11/14/sam-bankman-fried-broke-crypto-bank-for-dems/
56. https://dailyreckoning.com/biden-bucks-and-the-war-on-crypto/
57. https://medium.com/what-government-will-do-with-bitcoin/governments-can-and-will-attack-bitcoin-c8979c077577

1. **Go after the providers, the crypto wallets, and the exchanges.** *Make it impossible for the industry to focus and do business. That is happening right now. From The New York Times:*

   Government Cracks Down on Crypto Industry with Flurry of Actions

   "...the enforcement signals a growing urgency in Washington to address the threat posed by cryptocurrencies, an experimental technology that enables new forms of financial speculation. 'I've been referring to it as the crypto carpet bombing,' said Kristin Smith, the executive director of the Blockchain Association, a crypto industry trade group. 'Every couple hours we hear of some new enforcement action.'"[58]

2. **Prepare to classify bitcoin and all cryptocurrency as a "security," like a stock or bond, or a commodity, like wheat and soybeans, and don't treat it like money.** *This is also happening. And when it does, crypto becomes an investment of one type or another and not money, opening up multiple new layers for regulation and control. There are no laws restricting people of a certain income from holding money. But there are laws limiting access to investments by income.*

   According to Forbes:

   "The crypto crackdown could make it difficult for U.S. investors to trade their favorite digital currencies, and it threatens to undermine the decentralized nature that attracted many crypto investors in the first place."[59]

58. https://www.nytimes.com/2023/02/18/business/crypto-crackdown-regulation.html
59. https://www.forbes.com/advisor/investing/sec-crypto-regulation/

3. **If the government doesn't outright kill cryptocurrency, it will absolutely take its pound of flesh in the form of taxes.**[60] *That way the government can win regardless of what happens. It's pretty much what governments do, and it certainly can kill the crypto buzz.*

Bitcoin and cryptocurrency offer the promise of money as freedom. That is precisely why they are under assault. The Securities and Exchange Commission (SEC) went after Ripple (another cryptocurrency) in a big way recently.[61] Although Ripple won in court, the judge ruled that the government can regulate and control cryptocurrency if done with clarity.[62] The head of the SEC, Gary Gensler, has stated plainly that the "US Doesn't 'Need More Digital Currency' Because It Has the Dollar."[63] Uh…sure.

Central Bank Digital Currency (aka CBDC)

If not bitcoin, what does the government want? They want CONTROL and CBDC is how they plan to get it. We will dig in deep on this in Chapter Three but what you need to know is that this money will be the opposite of freedom. It's almost anti-money in that sense. And it is coming fast!

The Atlantic Council defines CBDC as "virtual money backed and issued by a central bank. As cryptocurrencies and stablecoins have become more popular, the world's central banks have realized that they need to provide an alternative—or let the future of money pass them by."[64]

60. https://www.bankrate.com/investing/crypto-taxes-guide-bitcoin-ethereum/
61. https://www.sec.gov/news/press-release/2020-338
62. https://techcrunch.com/2023/07/19/ripple-xrp-court-ruling
63. https://www-coindesk-com.cdn.ampproject.org/c/s/www.coindesk.com/policy/2023/06/06/us-doesnt-need-more-digital-currency-because-it-has-the-dollar-says-secs-gensler/
64. https://www.atlanticcouncil.org/cbdctracker/

Central Bank Digital Currencies are to bitcoin as Bizarro is to Superman. For those of you who did not waste your youth on comic books, Bizarro sort of looks like Superman and has his superpowers. But in reality, he is a failed clone and the opposite of the Man of Steel:

> *Bizarro is an inversion "of Superman with gray or chalk-white skin, a twisted sense of logic which typically manifests as a superficial 'opposite' of anything Superman would do or say and a resultant speech pattern ('Me am going to kill you' would mean 'I will save you' in Bizarro speech). Due to his imperfections, Bizarro is frequently a foe of Superman…"*[65]

Likewise, CBDC is the Bizarro bitcoin. It is digital and can function as money. Unlike bitcoin, it's not decentralized (instead controlled by the government), offers no privacy (actually exposes everything you do with it), and can be manufactured without limits. And, like Bizarro, it can prove very dangerous.

According to the Atlantic Council, 114 countries, representing 95% of the world's economy, are exploring CBDC and are at various stages of development.[66] They describe the path to development, a "Race for the Future of Money." This is coming whether we like it or not.

To better understand CBDC, let's review the Atlantic Council's overview found at https://www.atlanticcouncil.org/cbdctracker/:

The ABCs of CBDCs

What is a CBDC?

A Central Bank Digital Currency (CBDC) is the digital form of a country's fiat currency that is also a claim on the central bank. Instead of printing money, the central bank issues electronic coins or accounts backed by the full faith and credit of the government.

65. https://superman.fandom.com/wiki/Bizarro
66. https://www.atlanticcouncil.org/cbdctracker/

But don't digital currencies already exist?

There are already thousands of digital currencies, commonly called cryptocurrencies. Bitcoin is the most well-known fully decentralized cryptocurrency. Another type of cryptocurrency are stablecoins, whose value is pegged to an asset or a fiat currency like the dollar. Cryptocurrencies run on distributed-ledger technology, meaning that multiple devices all over the world, not one central hub, are constantly verifying the accuracy of the transaction. But this is different from a central bank issuing a digital currency.

So why would a government get into digital currencies?

There are many reasons to explore digital currencies, and the motivation of different countries for issuing CBDCs depends on their economic situation. Some common motivations are: promoting financial inclusion by providing easy and safer access to money for unbanked and underbanked populations; introducing competition and resilience in the domestic payments market, which might need incentives to provide cheaper and better access to money; increasing efficiency in payments and lowering transaction costs; creating programmable money and improving transparency in money flows; and providing for the seamless and easy flow of monetary and fiscal policy.

What are the challenges?

There are several challenges, and each one needs careful consideration before a country launches a CBDC. Citizens could pull too much money out of banks at once by purchasing CBDCs, triggering a run on banks—affecting their ability to lend and sending a shock to interest rates. This is especially a problem for countries with unstable financial systems. CBDCs also carry operational risks, since they are vulnerable to cyber attacks and need to be made resilient against them. Finally, CBDCs require a complex regulatory framework including privacy, consumer protection, and anti-money laundering standards which need to be made more robust before adopting this technology.

What are the national security implications of a CBDC?

New payments systems create externalities that impact the daily lives of citizens, and can possibly jeopardize the national security objectives of the country. They can, for example, limit the United States' ability to track cross-border flows and enforce sanctions. In the long term, the absence of US leadership and standards setting can have geopolitical consequences, especially if China and other countries maintain their first-mover advantage in the development of CBDCs. Our work on digital currencies at the GeoEconomics Center is at this nexus of the future of money and national security.

It's pretty clear that the Atlantic Council is a HUGE cheerleader for CBDC. They tout the benefits and justify everything from a government's perspective. They ignore the privacy and control risks. We will cover those in detail in Chapter Three and outline a plan for you to protect yourself in a later chapter. But it is important for you to know that most people see this as the future of money.

NOTE:

Don't get me wrong. CBDC could be a legitimate and Constitutional currency IF authorized by the Congress (not just an executive order) AND be fully exchangeable into gold and silver. Christopher P. Guzelian, Assistant Professor, Department of Finance and Economics, McCoy College of Business Administration, Texas State University, examined this question in detail.[67] His thoughts very much align with the proposal we put forth in this book. Unfortunately, I think he would agree that it is unlikely the Feds will heed his instruction as we will explain in Chapter Three.

67. https://papers.ssrn.com/sol3/papers.cfm?abstract_id=4400024

China's Golden Wallet

While we have been busy studying CBDC, the Chinese have been building their own version with Chinese characteristics.[68] Their goal goes beyond just having total currency control within their borders. Their goal is to displace the Western system entirely including killing the American dollar. They believe they must own the future of money and it absolutely will not be about your freedom. Quite the opposite, in fact.

China was the first nation to implement Social Credit Scores, allowing them to reward and punish citizens (or perhaps subjects) at will.[69] The enforcement mechanism is primarily economic and ultimately will be through China's version of CBDC, the Digital Yuan.[70] [The yuan is their version of our dollar.] At present, the Chinese Communist Party can monitor the activity of individuals. Anyone who steps out of line can be denied access to education or travel. But with the Digital Yuan, the CCP can have a line-item veto on personal spending. They can immediately extract fines. Or they can issue rewards.

The dangers of the Digital Yuan can be understood from a report produced by Cato Institute:

> *Alex Gladstein, chief strategy officer at the Human Rights Foundation, has recognized the danger to financial freedom and privacy inherent in central bank digital currency (CBDC), especially in repressive regimes like China. According to Gladstein, "The end of cash and the insta-analysis of financial transactions enable surveillance, state control, and, eventually, social engineering on a scale never thought possible." He points to China's social credit system, in conjunction with a digital*

68. https://www.scmp.com/comment/opinion/article/3219432/promotion-digital-yuan-will-serve-hong-kong-well-future
69. https://nhglobalpartners.com/china-social-credit-system-explained/
70. https://www.cato.org/blog/chinas-digital-yuan-threat-freedom

> *yuan, as paving the way toward "financial omniscience." Thus, "When the government can take financial privileges away for posting the wrong word on social media, saying the wrong thing in a call to parents, or sending the wrong photo to relatives, individuals self-censor and exercise extreme caution. In this way, control over money can create a social chilling effect."*
>
> *It is instructive, as Andrew Liu has reported in the Cato Journal, that government authorities have used regulations on mobile payments "to help the Communist Party maintain full political, social, and economic power," even though the official rhetoric is that those regulations were intended "to prevent criminal activity and improve mobile payment security." There is little doubt that Xi Jinping and his cadres in the State Council will be tempted to politicize the digital yuan to serve their own interests.*[71]

In many ways, the playbook for China is the same. Eliminate the competition and then full speed ahead. This is also made clear in the Cato report:

> *China has already cracked down on bitcoin, as well as other cryptocurrencies, to prevent circumvention of government control of money and banking, and to stem capital outflows. It is prudent to expect future crackdowns on e-CNY competitors and to expect an even greater concentration of political power.*

There are some critical differences between traditional CBDCs and China's Digital Yuan. Perhaps the most significant of these is that China has flirted with the idea of backing their currency with gold.[72] Although primarily rumors at this point, there is indication that China may be accumulating gold, along with Russia, building

71. Ibid
72. https://viewpoint.bnpparibas-am.com/renminbi-internationalisation-the-petro-yuan-and-the-role-of-gold/

reserves for that purpose.[73] Very recently, in fact, they began encouraging the Chinese people to make purchases of gold and store them with the government. They call it the "golden wallet."[74] It's sort of like our "pirate money" idea for Texas.[75] But watch out. They really are pirates! It will be easy to add gold to your wallet. Just don't count on getting it back out.

We will dive into the China threat to your money and how to beat it in Chapter Five.

Multinational Money

No discussion of the future of money would be complete without acknowledging the role of multinational groups. On the Eastern side, we have the BRICS nations (Brazil, Russia, India, China, South Africa, and now Saudi Arabia) and their large and growing sphere of influence. On the Western side, we have the International Monetary Fund (IMF), World Bank, and World Economic Forum.[76] Both hemispheres have become very active, very recently.

In regard to the IMF, they envision a one world platform under which all nations' CBDC would operate. According to Reuter's:

> *The International Monetary Fund (IMF) is working on a platform for central bank digital currencies (CDBCs) to enable transactions between countries, IMF Managing Director Kristalina Georgieva said on Monday.*

---

73. https://www.washingtontimes.com/news/2023/mar/6/russia-and-china-may-try-using-their-natural-resou/
74. https://www.zerohedge.com/news/2023-05-10/drainage-chinas-new-gold-wallet-may-suck-western-gold-dry
75. https://youtu.be/so2nqcbAakc
76. https://www.blacklistednews.com/article/84540/the-imf-has-just-unveiled-a-new-global-currency-known-as-the-universal-monetary-unit-that-is.html

> *"CBDCs should not be fragmented national propositions... To have more efficient and fairer transactions we need systems that connect countries: we need interoperability," Georgieva told a conference attended by African central banks in Rabat, Morocco.*
>
> *"For this reason, at the IMF, we are working on the concept of a global CBDC platform," she said.*
>
> *The IMF wants central banks to agree on a common regulatory framework for digital currencies that will allow global interoperability. Failure to agree on a common platform would create a vacuum that would likely be filled by cryptocurrencies, she said.*[77]

As if one nation's CBDC wasn't scary enough! **I have visions of the Galactic Empire and Darth Vader.** But that's just the Western version.

And in this corner, weighing in at a potential 30 countries, we have our challenger, the BRICS alliance. These mostly eastern emerging market nations have been working together for more than two decades. They formed an unlikely alliance based primarily on shared economic aspirations. Since at least 2008, however, those aspirations have included displacing the existing monetary system, primarily removing the U.S. dollar from its premier global position.[78] Now, they may be positioning to do just that.[79]

According to *Modern Diplomacy*, not only is the BRICS team growing, but it is also attracting a huge alliance of nations, including some major oil powerhouses:

---

77. https://www.reuters.com/markets/imf-working-global-central-bank-digital-currency-platform-2023-06-19/
78. https://globaleconomicwarfare.com/2014/07/replacing-the-western-financial-system-bric-by-brics/
79. https://foreignpolicy.com/2023/04/24/brics-currency-end-dollar-dominance-united-states-russia-china/

> *South Africa's representative to BRICS Ambassador Anil Sooklal has hinted that the grouping is set to grow bigger this year with more than 30 countries having formally and informally applied to join the alliance.*
>
> *The latest report indicates that the countries ready to join the BRICS alliance are Afghanistan, Algeria, Argentina, Bahrain, Bangladesh, Belarus, Egypt, Indonesia, Iran, Kazakhstan, Mexico, Nicaragua, Nigeria, Pakistan, Saudi Arabia, Senegal, Sudan, Syria, the United Arab Emirates, Thailand, Tunisia, Turkey, Uruguay, Venezuela, and Zimbabwe.*
>
> *The development will come as a blow to the United States of America and other Western nations, which will see their GDPs dwindle to that of the BRICS.*[80]

Instead of Darth Vader, I now get images of Ernst Blofeld, the James Bond villain intent on upending the global system as head of SPECTRE's international crime and terror cabal, taking control of all the energy in the world in order to control the money.[81] Or maybe they are the Trade Federation from Star Wars in keeping with the Darth Vader theme.[82]

It's important to remember that energy, especially crude oil, represents the #1 most traded product on the planet.[83] The oil trade has been a bedrock of the existing dollar-based monetary system for 50 years.[84] The BRICS alliance may be ready to challenge that.[85] To do so, they may be creating their own currency.[86] Jim Rickards says it will be the "biggest monetary shock in 52 years," and will drive

80. https://moderndiplomacy.eu/2023/05/24/more-than-30-countries-want-to-join-the-brics/
81. https://spywhothrills.com/blofeld
82. https://www.starwars.com/databank/trade-federation
83. https://oec.world/en/profile/hs/crude-petroleum
84. https://everything-everywhere.com/understanding-the-petrodollar-system/
85. https://www.cnbc.com/2023/06/14/china-and-saudi-arabia-are-part-of-a-multipolar-world-order-minister.html
86. https://pakobserver.net/and-now-the-brics-currency-by-rashid-ahmed-mughal/

gold prices higher.[87] Will a BRICS currency be the future of money? I sure hope not!

For me, I'm holding out for our own Texas (or any state) pirate money (gold and silver), made convenient with security and privacy. Arghhh!

Regardless, it is essential to understand that the current monetary system is under threat and how that will impact you. We'll learn about the domestic enemy in Chapter Three and the foreign enemy in Chapter Five.

87. https://www.zerohedge.com/markets/biggest-monetary-shock-52-years

It's A Trap!

—Admiral Ackbar, *Return of the Jedi*

3

BIDEN BUCKS

On March 9, 2022, President Biden issued Executive Order #14067.[88] It seemed innocuous enough. Sure, it was 37 pages long and had a lot of jargon, but it was exciting, especially to bitcoin fans who seemed thrilled that the government would finally take them seriously.[89] They had no idea it was poison-laced candy that really was a declaration of war on cryptocurrency and monetary privacy itself.[90] But it sounded good, at least at first.

The EO starts off with, "By the authority vested in me as president by the Constitutional laws of the United States, it is hereby ordered as follows…" It comes in nine Sections, with Section 1 described as policy. Here is the concluding paragraph that really telegraphs the story:

88. https://www.whitehouse.gov/briefing-room/presidential-actions/2022/03/09/executive-order-on-ensuring-responsible-development-of-digital-assets/
89. https://www.cnbc.com/2022/03/09/bitcoin-btc-jumps-after-treasury-statement-on-crypto-executive-order.html
90. https://coinchapter.com/bidens-executive-order-to-usher-in-the-3rd-great-dollar-earthquake/

> *The United States has an interest in responsible financial innovation, expanding access to safe and affordable financial services, and reducing the cost of domestic and cross-border funds transfers and payments, including through the continued modernization of public payment systems. We must take strong steps to reduce the risks that digital assets could pose to consumers, investors, and business protections; financial stability and financial system integrity; combating and preventing crime and illicit finance; national security;* ***the ability to exercise human rights; financial inclusion and equity; and climate change and pollution****.*[91]

Not bad till you get to that last part: *"the ability to exercise human rights; financial inclusion and equity; and climate change and pollution."* That's kind a lot to ask from your money, isn't it? Sure, I want innovation, affordability, convenience. I want stability, integrity, and safety. But is my money supposed to deliver human rights, financial inclusion, equity, and halt climate change???? That is simply forcing on you the woke principles of ESG and DEI.[92] How does that fit in there?

And that is the point. Money should be neutral, not political. And the Biden team views a digital currency as a means to enforce woke political policy. They aren't even hiding it and that is frightening! We already have to deal with our corporations, retailers, media, social media, government, library, pensions, churches, schools, and even our beer cramming down wokeness 24/7.[93] But now our money?

You can switch the beer you drink. You can change banks. You can watch alternative media. But you can't simply choose a different currency. At least not yet. No wonder the severe crackdown on

91. https://www.whitehouse.gov/briefing-room/presidential-actions/2022/03/09/executive-order-on-ensuring-responsible-development-of-digital-assets/
92. https://www.heritage.org/progressivism/commentary/what-wrong-esg-wokeism
93. https://www.washingtonexaminer.com/restoring-america/community-family/the-real-reason-beer-companies-are-going-woke

bitcoin. The Feds are eliminating the competition! You can see that when you read the full order and then watch the government agencies spring into action, taking down the crypto industry piece by piece.

And That's Not the Scary Part

There have been dozens of reports on how America could implement CBDC, aka "Biden Bucks." Some of the more important of these are 1) the White House Office of Science and Technology (*Technical Possibilities for a U.S. Central Bank Digital Currency*, September 2022)[94], 2) a Treasury Department Report (*The Future of Money and Payments*, September 2022),[95] 3) FEDS Notes from the Federal Reserve (*Programmable Money*, June 2021),[96] and 4) the International Monetary Fund's report (*The Money Revolution*, September 2022).[97]

The bottom line? Consider this from my friend Justin Haskins (author with Glenn Beck of *The Great Reset: Joe Biden and the Rise of 21st Century Fascism*),[98] writing for Fox News:

> *Under the leadership of President Joe Biden, the White House and the Federal Reserve have started to lay the groundwork for a programmable, trackable, easily manipulated digital currency. It might sound like something from a dystopian science-fiction novel, but it's all too real, and it could soon change life in America forever…*
>
> *A CBDC would not be a digital version of the existing paper-based dollar, but rather an entirely new currency that would exist exclusively in a digital (meaning an electronic, non-physical) form…*

94. https://www.whitehouse.gov/wp-content/uploads/2022/09/09-2022-Technical-Evaluation-US-CBDC-System.pdf
95. https://home.treasury.gov/system/files/136/Future-of-Money-and-Payments.pdf
96. https://www.federalreserve.gov/econres/notes/feds-notes/what-is-programmable-money-20210623.html
97. https://www.imf.org/-/media/Files/Publications/Fandd/Article/2022/September/fd090122.ashx
98. https://www.amazon.com/Great-Reset-Biden-Twenty-First-Century-Fascism/dp/B09RRNW7XF/

Since the flurry of action in September, the administration has worked tirelessly – and quietly – to advance the creation of a CBDC, through various working groups, speeches and coordinated efforts with non-government groups.

Under the various CBDC proposals floated by the Biden administration and Federal Reserve, a U.S. CBDC would be programmable, traceable and designed to promote various left-wing social goals, such as improving "financial inclusion" and "equity." It would also be designed to help with "transitioning to a net-zero emissions economy and improving environmental justice." . . .

Additionally, because a CBDC would be digital and programmable, rules could be imposed that limit spending on approved activities. So, if the federal government or Federal Reserve were to determine that Americans are buying too much gasoline, for example, it could stop people from using CBDCs at gas stations with a few clicks on a computer.

Perhaps most disturbing of all, however, is that under most of the CBDC designs discussed by the Biden administration and Federal Reserve, nearly all forms of ownership of CBDC money would also be strictly limited. Only large institutions such as banks, the federal government, and/or the Federal Reserve would actually have ownership of CBDCs. Everyone else would be prevented from having absolute control over their digital money.

If a programmable CBDC is rolled out in the near future, you won't own money and you'll have very little privacy, if any at all. That's great news for those who advocate for bigger government and want more power for large financial institutions, but it could prove to be a catastrophic loss of freedom for the rest of us.[99]

99. https://www.foxnews.com/opinion/biden-administration-quietly-planning-future-where-you-dont-own-money

This is an Administration with an agenda. So, when they push forward a currency that the Federal Reserve itself describes as "programmable money," WATCH OUT! I'd say, "watch your wallets," but if Biden gets his way, you won't have a wallet! Not a physical one anyway.

This is the same Administration that wants to make mortgages less expensive to those with lower credit scores and more expensive to those with better credit.[100] Again, it is Bizarro! They see money as programmable so they can reward those who line up with their social goals and punish those who refuse. Don't believe me? PayPal already signaled a similar scheme when they floated the idea of fining any customers caught "spreading misinformation" on the Internet.[101] When you realize that even truth can be construed as misinformation if it goes against official government narrative, you get the idea.[102] Money can be used as a weapon to stifle freedom.[103] That's the opposite of what it should do!

Sadly, using programmable money to control your speech is just the tip of a very big iceberg. It doesn't come close to stopping there as CBDC is the ultimate control mechanism for your behavior as well. Think of it as a "line-item veto" on your spending. What if the government decides you should not own a gas-powered stove?[104] They can ban them outright or better yet, with CBDC, simply prevent the purchase.[105] Imagine going to Home Depot and attempting to pay for a new JennAir range. When you start to pay, the clerk says, "sorry but you have been declined." Others who have been less vocal on the Internet might see their purchase go through, however. This is

100. https://www.cbsnews.com/miami/news/mortgage-rate-changes-to-benefit-those-with-lower-credit-scores/

101. https://www.washingtonpost.com/politics/2022/10/10/paypal-faces-backlash-after-floating-fines-sharing-misinformation/

102. https://www.washingtontimes.com/news/2023/mar/5/covid-19-conspiracy-theories-turned-out-to-be-true/

103. https://www.wnd.com/2023/05/u-s-may-freeze-bank-withdrawals-currency-fear-rises-expert-warns/

104. https://www.theepochtimes.com/bidens-green-rules-mean-appliances-will-soon-cost-more-and-do-less-experts-say_5301671.html

105. https://newhouse.house.gov/media/weekly-columns-and-op-eds/ban-gas-stoves-just-beginning

just like China's Social Credit Score system. And that's the point! Even Klaus Schwab, Dr. Evil of the World Economic Forum, agrees. He declares that "China is a model for many nations."[106]

What if you want to buy gas for your car? CBDC will know how many gallons you've bought this month or how many miles you've driven and decide whether or not you can.[107] Remember, they want to phase out all gasoline.[108] But I'll bet Biden will get all the gas he wants for his classic Corvette.

What if you want to travel? Only if you have been good, as defined by the Biden Administration. Otherwise, you are limited to a 15-minute radius of your home.[109] Your money simply stops working outside your zip code.

Want to buy a gun? Forget it![110] You may have a Second Amendment right to bear arms, but your money just might not let you buy one.

Want a cheeseburger? CBDC controllers can check your latest cholesterol scores and see if that's OK. But vegan fake meat is fine. Or maybe a salad. Think I'm exaggerating? Don't forget that the mayor of New York tried to limit the size of soda you could purchase. That was more than 10 years ago.[111] Think the ruling elite has gotten less

106. https://www.foxnews.com/world/world-economic-forum-chair-klaus-schwab-declares-chinese-state-tv-china-model-many-nations
107. https://texasscorecard.com/state/republicans-join-democrats-pushing-mileage-tax-for-texas-drivers/
108. https://www.reuters.com/world/us/biden-pledges-end-gas-powered-federal-vehicle-purchases-by-2035-2021-12-08/
109. https://www.theepochtimes.com/15-minute-cities-are-complete-impoverishment-and-enslavement-of-all-the-people_5231593.html
110. https://reason.com/2023/03/06/banks-increasingly-back-political-scheme-to-track-gun-purchases-by-credit-card/
111. https://www.nytimes.com/2012/05/31/nyregion/bloomberg-plans-a-ban-on-large-sugared-drinks.html

"nanny state" since then? Oh, and don't forget how bad meat is for the climate. Cows emit methane, by the way. Better to eat bugs.[112]

Programmable money can go even further, and the government is salivating over the control. What if you want to give to the wrong political candidate? Think the ruling elite (that investigated Trump as a candidate at the request of his opponent based on doctored opposition research, impeached him twice, raided his home, and brought multiple criminal charges) would let you support him as a candidate?[113] Or maybe you want to give to the wrong church or charity? Bad behavior gets punished.

What if you have the wrong skin color or heritage?[114] Or are you "cisgender?" Maybe your money should be worth less than those who have been underprivileged. We won't need a wealth tax or reparations, just programmable money to set things right.[115]

And don't forget that "undesirables" (as defined by the government) can lose their bank account entirely. Being debanked is the newest threat of punishment to keep people in line.[116,117]

The Canadian Justice Minister (akin to our Attorney General) under Trudeau let the plans slip during the Trucker Freedom Convoy. You may remember that truckers were protesting vaccine mandates and lockdowns in 2022 as the Canadian government turned increasingly draconian.[118] When Truckers protested, the government swiftly moved against them AND anyone who supported them. From the *Toronto Sun*:

112. https://www.science.org/content/article/fight-global-warming-eat-bugs
113. https://republicbrief.com/furious-business-puts-up-sign-saying-no-sales-to-trump-supporters/
114. https://townhall.com//tipsheet/leahbarkoukis/2023/06/07/south-africa-water-for-white-people-n2624088
115. https://www.thegatewaypundit.com/2023/06/new-california-law-will-base-electricity-bills-income/
116. https://adflegal.org/article/debanking-cancel-cultures-newest-threat
117. https://www.wnd.com/2023/06/u-k-debanks-conservative-commentator-british-equivalent-tucker-carlson
118. https://www.wsj.com/articles/freedom-convoy-canada-trucker-protest-what-11644441237

> *David Lametti says if you're part of a "Pro-Trump movement" you should "be worried" about your bank account being frozen by the Government . . .*
>
> *The Trudeau Liberals have used the Emergencies Act to greatly expand the power of the government to monitor financial transactions, expanding existing cryptocurrencies like Bitcoin. They have also increased the responsibilities of financial institutions to report transactions.*
>
> *The declaration of emergency goes so far as to "require any financial service provider to determine whether they have in their possession or control property that belongs to a person who participates in the blockade." That could see the bank accounts of people who attended the protest but didn't fund them frozen at the direction of the government.*[119]

Oh, but that's Canada. Couldn't happen here. Unless you look at the official FDIC policy known as "Operation Choke Point" that was intended to debank undesirables like gun sellers and payday loan companies. My friend, the Honorable Frank Keating, former Governor of Oklahoma, and former president of the American Bankers Association, explained this in a writeup published in *The Hill*:

> *A little-known program carried out by President Obama's Department of Justice (DOJ) whipsawed small business for years, and to date no one has been held accountable. Federal officials pressured banks to close the accounts of businesses solely because they were ideologically opposed to their existence. This runs counter to the very principles of due process and fairness that form the backbone of our nation's laws.*

119. https://torontosun.com/news/national/trudeau-minister-threatens-to-seize-accounts-of-pro-trump-convoy-donors

> *This program, known as Operation Choke Point, operated unrestrained for years. Officials at both the Comptroller of the Currency (OCC) and the Federal Deposit Insurance Corporation (FDIC) threatened banks with regulatory pressure if they did not bend to their will. Gun and ammunition dealers, payday lenders and other businesses operating legally suddenly found banks terminating their accounts with little explanation aside from "regulatory pressure." . . .*
>
> *What's more, recently unsealed documents show the FDIC and OCC put banks in an untenable position. As the former president of the American Bankers Association, I am appalled at the brazen threats levied against banks during Operation Choke Point. In one case, the FDIC's Atlanta Regional Office met with a bank chairman and suggested he would face criminal prosecution if he did not terminate the bank's relationship with a payday lender. Banks should answer to federal and state law, not to the whims of individual regulators with a vendetta against lawful businesses.*

In addition to all of that, conservatives are seemingly debanked on purely ideological grounds.[120] How else can you explain the "secret and irrevocable" closing of accounts for the National Committee for Religious Freedom headed by former Senator and Ambassador Sam Brownback?[121] No explanation. Just, "your business is not welcome here."[122]

Then, there's my friend Nick Vujicic. Born without arms or legs, Nick has devoted much of his life to helping young people cope, overcome depression, find life worth living, reject suicide, and discover Christ. Really, there's no individual more sympathetic, more talented, or

120. https://washingtonstand.com/news/experts-point-to-pattern-of-conservatives-being-debanked
121. https://www.christianpost.com/news/religious-nonprofit-group-says-chase-closed-its-bank-account.html
122. https://www.dailywire.com/news/jpmorgan-chase-denies-they-debanked-religious-groups-head-of-impacted-nonprofit-responds

nicer than Nick. And yet, he was debanked without explanation.[123]

No wonder people are concerned that some governments now require you to provide your social media handles when opening bank accounts:

> *In its recently released Customer Due Diligence Regulations, 2023, Nigeria's apex bank said money deposit banks must obtain comprehensive information about their customers, including their social media handles...The new regulation states, in part, that; "By including social media handles as part of the customer identification process, banks seek to gain further insights into customers' online presence and activities, helping to assess potential risks and monitor for suspicious behaviour.*[124]

Nothing creepy about that!

Bottom line? If you support something that government doesn't like, or if you are just curious enough to show up at a Freedom Rally, or maybe just tweet the wrong thing, you could lose your bank account. But that's just version 1.0 of the control scheme. With CBDC, even if you are allowed to keep your account, the money in it can be tracked and turned off at the whim of a bureaucrat. Was the Trudeau government acting rogue?[125] No, actually. Trudeau has been shown to be a lapdog for both Klaus Schwab (World Economic

123. https://xotv.me/channels/233-economic-war-room/vod_videos/15106-man-with-no-arms-or-legs-gets-de-banked-are-you-next-guest-nick-vujicic-ep-213
124. https://www.premiumtimesng.com/news/top-news/606589-cbn-mandates-banks-to-scrutinise-customers-social-media-presence-as-serap-kicks.html
125. https://www.spiked-online.com/2023/04/27/can-justin-trudeaus-canada-get-any-more-authoritarian/

Forum)[126] and Xi Jinping (Chinese Communist Party).[127] Even the United Nations, with support from Iran, North Korea, and China, pushes for demonetizing anyone who engages in hate speech, mis- or disinformation as they define it.[128] They wrote an entire 28-page report, OUR COMMON AGENDA POLICY BRIEF 8: INFORMATION INTEGRITY ON DIGITAL PLATFORMS, explaining why and how to censor those who oppose their narrative by demonetizing them.[129]

> *Strengthening information integrity on digital platforms is an urgent priority for the international community. From* ***health and gender equality to peace, justice, education and climate action****, measures that limit the impact of mis- and dis- information and hate speech will boost efforts to achieve a sustainable future and leave no one behind. Even with action at the national level, these problems can only be fully addressed through stronger global cooperation.*[130]

This is simply where the world is headed.[131]

A Conspiracy Theory?

I know, this sounds like "tin foil hat" stuff. Or dystopian science fiction. But it's not. In fact, the elite discuss it openly and are planning everything I've shared. They act like this is right and normal the same way they say with a straight face that three-year-olds should be allowed to choose their gender and undergo permanent life-altering

126. https://nationalpost.com/news/canada/first-reading-does-the-wef-secretly-control-the-canadian-government
127. https://theconversation.com/why-did-xi-scold-trudeau-maybe-because-canada-spent-years-helping-china-erode-human-rights-194899
128. https://www.wnd.com/2023/06/now-u-n-wants-demonetize-everyone-speaks-real-truth/
129. https://www.un.org/sites/un2.un.org/files/our-common-agenda-policy-brief-information-integrity-en.pdf
130. Ibid, page 25
131. https://www.bitchute.com/video/Qkx35gWR8afi/

surgery.[132] At the Summer Davos meeting in China, one speaker (Eswar Prasad), openly bragged that CBDC could be used to eliminate sales of ammunition (or anything the government found undesirable).[133] To prove the point, computer analysts recently cracked the Brazilian CBDC source code and discovered that this capability really was there.[134]

Investopedia "says the quiet part out loud" in their article titled, "Why Governments Seek to Eliminate Cash" (May 23, 2023):

> *Digital transactions or electronic money create an audit trail for law enforcement and financial institutions and can aid governments in economic policymaking. Transactions using digital money reduce costs and create transparency in an individual's spending and savings habits.*
>
> *Since 2016, global policies have been implemented to thwart the use of cash in favor of digital currency transactions. In the United States, any financial institution that receives a cash deposit of more than $10,000 must report it to the IRS, making tracing illegal activity easier.*
>
> *Promoting and tracking digital transactions amounts to a war on cash. The use of digital money avoids the use of cash as transactions are handled by computers and the internet. Critics argue that limiting the use of cash and forcing individuals to pay through banks or credit card companies compromise financial privacy, prevent interest accumulation on saved cash, and limit profits of small business owners who often rely on cash sales.*[135]

---

132. https://www.kqed.org/futureofyou/440851/can-you-really-know-that-a-3-year-old-is-transgender
133. https://sociable.co/government-and-policy/governments-program-cbdc-restrict-undesirable-purchases-wef-summer-davos-china/
134. https://cryptonews.com/news/brazilian-central-bank-digital-currency-raises-alarm-as-developer-uncovers-fund-freezing-feature.htm
135. https://www.investopedia.com/articles/investing/021816/why-governments-want-eliminate-cash.asp

Investopedia is as mainstream as you get, and they state the obvious here. But that's the point. This is a nefarious plot in plain sight! CBDC is a means to monitor and ultimately control spending and behavior.

Cato Institute said it plainly in a July 18, 2022, commentary: "Central Bank Digital Currencies and Freedom Are Incompatible."[136] Here are a few thoughts they included:

1. **CBDC would allow the government to take money from your account at will.**
   (Former IMF official Eswar) Prasad, now a professor of trade policy and economics at Cornell University, gave a blunt assessment of how CBDCs will affect monetary policy:

   One should recognize that the CBDC creates new opportunity for monetary policy. If we all had CBDC accounts instead of cash, in principle it might be possible to implement negative interest rates simply by shrinking balances in CBDC accounts. It will become a lot easier to undertake helicopter drops of money. If everybody had a CBDC account, you could easily increase the balance in those accounts.

   Prasad's "helicopter drops of money" informed the article title, but the flip side of CBDC helicopter money is the real attention getter. It's right there in plain sight: shrinking balances in CBDC accounts to implement negative interest rates...

   At its core, this brave new world of monetary policy equates to the government saying that your money isn't really your money. Your property rights are subservient to the "public good" and the supposed necessity of "managing the national economy."

   In other words, central banks will take money out of people's accounts to conduct monetary policy.

136. https://www.cato.org/commentary/central-bank-digital-currencies-freedom-are-incompatible

2. **CBDC is designed to protect the government's power at your expense.**
   The truth is CBDCs are government's attempt to protect its privileged position and exert more control over people's money.

   But money itself is not a public good. The fact that its production has been increasingly encroached upon by the government does not make it a public good. And the fact that something called a CBDC even exists is owed only to payment innovations that occurred in the private market.

3. **CBDC would allow the government complete control over your life.**
   The real danger in CBDCs is that there is no limit to the level of control that the government could exert over people if money is purely electronic and provided directly by the government. A CBDC would give federal officials full control over the money going into–and coming out of–every person's account.

   This level of government control is not compatible with economic or political freedom.

This gets us back to the original point. Money is supposed to be freedom. But this Bizarro version is exactly the opposite. It means money becomes slavery.

If CBDC is That Bad, Why Would You Ever Use It?

One of my best friends is Dr. Erik Davidson, a finance professor at Baylor University. He was a colleague when we both worked at Templeton, best man at my wedding, a former business partner, and brother in Christ.[137] I love him dearly and admire him even more, if that's possible. Yet, he once joked with me that he was afraid he

137. https://hankamer.baylor.edu/person/erik-h-davidson

might inadvertently take "the mark of the beast."[138] To a believing Christian, this would be the ultimate mistake. The concept comes from the 13th Chapter of the book of the Revelation, the final book in the Bible (verses 11-18 from NKJV):

> [11] *Then I saw another beast coming up out of the earth, and he had two horns like a lamb and spoke like a dragon.* [12] *And he exercises all the authority of the first beast in his presence, and causes the earth and those who dwell in it to worship the first beast, whose deadly wound was healed.* [13] *He performs great signs, so that he even makes fire come down from heaven on the earth in the sight of men.* [14] *And he deceives [f]those who dwell on the earth by those signs which he was granted to do in the sight of the beast, telling those who dwell on the earth to make an image to the beast who was wounded by the sword and lived.* [15] *He was granted power to give breath to the image of the beast, that the image of the beast should both speak and cause as many as would not worship the image of the beast to be killed.* [16] *He causes all, both small and great, rich and poor, free and slave, to receive a mark on their right hand or on their foreheads,* [17] *and that no one may buy or sell except one who has the mark or the name of the beast, or the number of his name.* [18] *Here is wisdom. Let him who has understanding calculate the number of the beast, for it is the number of a man: His number is 666.*

Then, in Chapter 14 (verses 9-11 NKJV), the Bible explains why taking the mark is such a bad idea:

138. https://www.crossway.org/articles/what-is-the-mark-of-the-beast-revelation-13/

[9] Then a third angel followed them, saying with a loud voice, "If anyone worships the beast and his image, and receives his mark on his forehead or on his hand, [10] he himself shall also drink of the wine of the wrath of God, which is poured out full strength into the cup of His indignation. He shall be tormented with fire and brimstone in the presence of the holy angels and in the presence of the Lamb. [11] And the smoke of their torment ascends forever and ever; and they have no rest day or night, who worship the beast and his image, and whoever receives the mark of his name."

Scary stuff! I couldn't imagine a true believer ever accepting the mark knowing that. So, I asked Erik why he fears he might take it. He (jokingly) shared that it would probably be offered in an email advertisement with the promise of frequent flyer miles. Two clicks of a mouse and he's marked for eternity. His joke makes a point. People do a lot of stuff without understanding the implications. And that will certainly be the case with accepting CBDC.

It will start voluntarily as a benefit. Maybe the next stimulus package will require that you open an account to get the "free" money offered to help in the next financial crisis. Some will be stubborn and refuse it. Eventually, the holdouts will be deemed a threat to society, supporting criminal activity, or something like that. Then, it becomes mandatory.

That's how they went from the offering of "freedom" in the form of a voluntary Covid vaccine for the privileged[139] to slavery in the form of a mandate within months.[140] If the government had its way, you would not have been able to work (earn money) or shop (spend money) unless you were fully up to date on your shots.[141]

139. https://www.statnews.com/2020/12/03/how-rich-and-privileged-can-skip-the-line-for-covid19-vaccines/
140. https://www.aafp.org/pubs/fpm/blogs/gettingpaid/entry/health_care_staff_vaccination.html
141. https://news.bloomberglaw.com/daily-labor-report/vaccine-mandates-at-work-part-of-new-normal-employers-say

The next crisis may not be a health pandemic. Instead, it may be a financial crisis and it could be coming faster than you might believe (as we will explain in the next chapter).

One of the most disturbing things about CBDC is how nonchalant people can be about it.[142] It's true that only 16% really want CBDC and most are skeptical.[143] But some see it as convenience without counting the cost.[144] Others see it as an exciting new tech opportunity that may make them rich.[145] Some say that Congress will never pass it even though a version is winding through Congress now.[146] Or, could the authority of the Fed already granted by Congress be sufficient?[147] Even among those who are concerned, many believe they can stop CBDC at the state or local level or in the courts. That is very naïve.

The truth is that the machine behind implementing CBDC is already in place. Banks, retailers, federal agencies, the Federal Reserve, the Treasury Department, the rich and powerful, media, social media, and payment processors are already on board waiting for the trigger to be pulled.

A few brave states (God bless 'em) have taken action to outlaw CBDC.[148,149] I hope they succeed but fear they won't.[150] The problem is that the Constitution outlines monetary authority in Article 1, Section 8 (clause 5):

142. https://www.omfif.org/2022/04/how-real-is-the-cbdc-threat-to-privacy/
143. https://www.cato.org/survey-reports/poll-only-16-americans-support-government-issuing-central-bank-digital-currency
144. https://cointelegraph.com/news/cz-on-central-bank-digital-currencies-the-more-we-have-the-better
145. https://www.centralbanking.com/awards/7958962/the-winners-of-the-2023-fintech-regtech-global-awards
146. https://thehill.com/opinion/congress-blog/4035602-are-congressional-republicans-about-to-greenlight-a-cbdc/
147. https://rollcall.com/2022/10/18/can-congress-buy-in-to-digital-dollar-without-legislation/
148. https://decrypt.co/140505/ron-desantis-banned-cbdcs-in-florida-these-states-could-be-next
149. https://watcher.guru/news/texas-introduces-bill-to-ban-central-bank-digital-currency-cdbc
150. https://www.politico.com/newsletters/digital-future-daily/2023/03/23/states-challenge-washington-over-the-future-of-money-00088608

The Congress shall have Power . . . To coin Money, regulate the Value thereof, and of foreign Coin, and fix the Standard of Weights and Measures. . .[151]

Unfortunately, that is pretty clear. Constitutional scholars all agree that Congress (and through an act of Congress the Federal Reserve) has ultimate authority over money in America. States are specifically prohibited from coining money. [Although they can allow pirate money as we will soon see.]

Think the courts will stop CBDC? Remember that these same courts allowed fiat money.[152] Absolutely, it is a bastardization of Founders' intent. They didn't want unlimited paper money printed at will and backed by nothing.[153] You think the Founders intended a privately owned Federal Reserve to have complete control over our money and economy? Of course not. The Founders feared paper money, knowing the control it would give to the elite. But the courts have allowed and even endorsed it, viewing money as an enumerated power of the Congress. CBDC is a trillion times worse! But if Congress allows it (or even fails to stop it), the courts will likely allow it as well.

As for the states, they will eventually be at the complete mercy of the Feds (unless they do something amazing). As a kid (back when I could get a candy bar for a dime and when Nixon ended the gold standard), I remember the battle over a nationwide 55-mile-per-hour speed limit.[154] Boastful local politicians swore that it would never happen in their state! "The Federal government has no jurisdiction," they would say.[155] But then the Congress threatened to withhold highway funds and one by one, they caved.[156] Money talks. In the case of CBDC, money shouts. It shouts so loudly that all other voices

151. https://constitution.congress.gov/browse/article-1/section-8/
152. https://idahofreedom.org/fighting-the-feds-digital-dollar-a-free-market-solution/
153. https://www.nationalreview.com/2011/07/founders-no-fans-paper-currency-deroy-murdock/
154. https://groovyhistory.com/55-mph-speed-limit/4
155. https://www.gao.gov/assets/ced-77-27.pdf
156. https://www.latimes.com/archives/la-xpm-1989-09-01-mn-1474-story.html

could be silenced. Imagine if the Feds attempted to turn off a state's CBDC money with the same determination they did with highway funds? Who would stop them?

Look out for the trap! Money, which is supposed to mean freedom, could soon become the shackles of slavery.

The good news? We have an answer, and you can help bring it to pass...Keep reading! It will get worse, then much, much better. You'll see. We have a way out of the trap, and it all depends on modern pirate money.

Pirate Money

Never let a serious crisis go to waste.
—Rahm Emanuel

4

The Coming Storm and The Great Reset

Another thing I loved as a kid was the board game Monopoly. I always wanted the race car but would settle for the top hat. I hated being stuck with the purse or the thimble. It didn't really matter, though. I loved Monopoly. When we traveled to London, I bought the UK version at Hamleys Toy Shop, the world's oldest and largest toy store.[157, 158] Instead of Boardwalk and Park Place, it had Mayfair and Park Lane. Otherwise, it played the same. My collection grew over time and even purchased a Russian-language edition of the classic Parker Brother's game.[159] I found it with pieces still in shrink wrap on the shelf of a closet, never played because I can't read Russian.

One thing that every Monopoly fan knows, though, is that oftentimes games don't end with a clear victory. Instead, a player who is bored,

157. https://www.hamleys.com/monopoly-classic-game
158. https://londranews.com/english/hamleys-in-london-the-largest-toy-store-in-the-world
159. https://artsandculture.google.com/asset/board-game-monopoly-russian-language-edition-parker-brothers/tQFDmBPK_sfjog

vindictive, or just a bad loser will flip the board and ruin the game. In fact, that probably happens more often than a fair game played out. The board also gets flipped when one or more players are caught cheating. They flip the board to cover their tracks.

KEVIN 'S MONOPOLY GAME COLLECTION.

We are about to see those who have been manipulating everything flip the board in real life. Economic reality has exposed their cheating, so they plan to reset the board for their own advantage. Unlike with a game, though, you can't just pick up the pieces and go home. You'll be forced to play as they change the rules, take over all the properties, and control the bank. And you'll never get the race car. It will be thimbles for everyone.

This is, in short, The Great Reset. And it is here. Now.[160]

160. https://imprimis.hillsdale.edu/what-is-the-great-reset/

Why the Board Will be Flipped

The truth is hard. The game is almost over. When Nixon left the gold standard in 1971, our government had total reported Federal debt of about $400 billion.[161] It was under $1 trillion when Reagan took office, a little over $10 trillion when President Obama was elected, and about $20 trillion when Trump was elected. Now we are well past $32 trillion and by my estimate may exceed $50 trillion before this decade is out.[162] The game is over, and the board will soon be flipped.

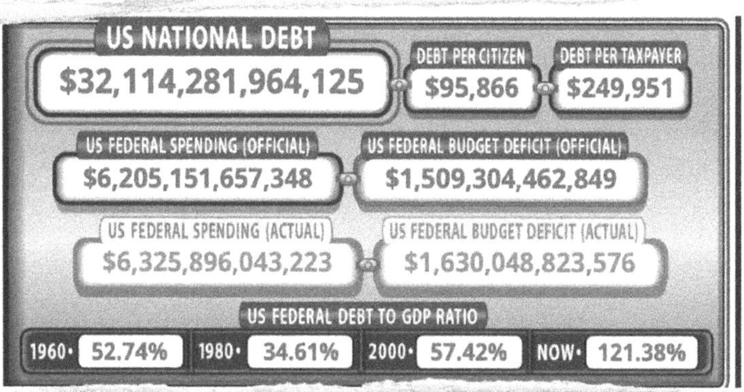

https://www.usdebtclock.org/index.html, accessed June 24, 2023

I've studied this problem in great detail for quite a while. In fact, I was hired by the state of Utah back in early 2016 to do an economic risk analysis. You can read the report at https://le.utah.gov/interim/2016/pdf/00001792.pdf. At the time, we had less than $20 trillion in reported Federal debt. But the trajectory was obvious and the conclusions stark. We were headed to a major financial crisis unless we reduced spending, increased income, or both. If we didn't alter the path, I predicted the demise of the dollar system.

161. https://www.thebalancemoney.com/national-debt-by-year-compared-to-gdp-and-major-events-3306287
162. https://www.usdebtclock.org/index.html

Sadly, despite presenting the facts and an action plan, my warnings remain unheeded.

What the elites know, while the rest of us seem to go blindly on assuming what has been always will be, is that our current debt-based economy is unsustainable. We can't get the government to stop excessive spending. They won't even slow down. Politicians love to spend your money. And your kid's money. And that of your grandchildren. But they don't want you to feel the pinch, so they are slow to raise taxes. That's how they cheat. But reality has a way of showing up and it's about to make an appearance.

Until very recently, central banks around the world cheated the game by taking interest rates close to zero. In some cases, bankers enforced "negative interest rates" where you actually paid them to borrow your money. Hard to wrap your head around this, but it happened and in a big way, reaching over $18 trillion in 2020.[163] Then came reality in the form of inflation.

Negative interest rates were only for the benefit of governments, big corporations, and the wealthy. The rest of us still had to pay to borrow money, sometimes at exorbitant rates. But savers and those on fixed incomes were left with little to no return for their hard-earned money. Speculators got wealthy using essentially free money. In short, the rich got richer while the rest of us struggled.[164]

Inevitably, inflation returned, forcing interest rates higher. At first, the Fed said it was transitory so they could keep rates lower for longer. We knew differently and said so.[165] We saw clear signs that the board was about to be flipped. When headline inflation hit a 40-year high,

163. https://www.bloomberg.com/news/articles/2020-12-11/world-s-negative-yield-debt-pile-at-18-trillion-for-first-time#xj4y7vzkg
164. https://www.economist.com/finance-and-economics/2020/10/15/low-interest-rates-leave-savers-with-few-good-options
165. https://globaleconomicwarfare.com/2021/02/the-coming-inflation-and-what-it-means-for-you/

the Federal Reserve was forced to act.[166] Interest rates that had been held near zero were now targeted to be over 5% as shown in the FRED chart from the St. Louis Federal Reserve.[167]

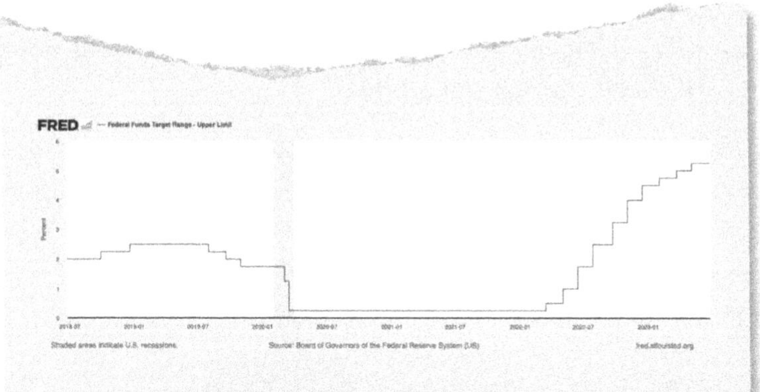

INTEREST RATES 2018 – 2023

Let's do a little math.

In 2021, the total interest our government paid was $352 billion, about 1.3% of the $28 trillion they owed.[168] But what happens when debt increases to $32 trillion and interest rates go to 5.25% as the Fed is now targeting? Net interest expense rises to $1.68 trillion, nearly a five-fold increase.

Did you know that the total of ALL personal income tax (not payroll taxes) is just a little over $2.4 trillion per year?[169] That means that at fair-market rates, net interest on our government debt would consume 70% of all personal income tax receipts. That is unsustainable and the Congressional Budget Office, General

166. https://www.businessinsider.com/inflation-report-cpi-september-prices-rent-fed-rates-recession-outlook-2022-10
167. https://fred.stlouisfed.org/series/DFEDTARU#0
168. https://www.pgpf.org/blog/2023/02/interest-costs-on-the-national-debt-are-on-track-to-reach-a-record-high
169. https://www.usdebtclock.org/index.html accessed June 23, 2024

Accounting Office, and even Biden's Treasury Department admit it.[170,171,172,173] And yet, the government is incurring an additional $1.7 trillion of deficit spending this year which will, all other things being equal, lead to higher rates. So why did the Republicans cave in the budget showdown?[174] An unwillingness to face reality or the sad fact that a Uniparty runs our government?[175] Perhaps it doesn't matter. The fiscal cliff was not averted.

I can remember when the government had to pay 10% to borrow money. In fact, the Fed Funds rate was once almost 20% when Jimmy Carter was leaving office.[176] If that happened today, we'd be wiped out as a nation. Yet, the elites keep playing, pretending nothing is wrong, but fully aware the board will be flipped soon.[177]

NOTE:

By the way, have you ever considered that the Federal Reserve has a monopoly on money? Doesn't that make the bills and notes they produce "Monopoly money?"[178] *It's kind of funny because a few years back, Parker Brothers introduced an all-electronic version of Monopoly where you no longer used paper bills, just electronic debits and credits.*[179] *Foreshadowing of CBDC and a cashless society? I never owned that edition, but I did see they also made a Pirate Version. If it has doubloons and pieces of eight, I might need to get a copy of that one from eBay for my collection!*[180]

170. https://www.cbo.gov/publication/58946
171. https://www.gao.gov/products/gao-23-106201
172. https://www.fiscal.treasury.gov/reports-statements/financial-report/unsustainable-fiscal-path.html
173. https://www.washingtonexaminer.com/policy/economy/cbo-projects-debt-107-percent-gdp-2029
174. https://rollcall.com/2023/05/31/the-ultimate-no-win-debt-deal-for-mccarthy-house-republicans/
175. https://www.conservapedia.com/Uniparty
176. https://www.bankrate.com/banking/federal-reserve/history-of-federal-funds-rate/
177. https://xotv.me/channels/233-economic-war-room/vod_videos/13920-why-you-need-an-economic-war-room-are-you-ready-for-the-next-crisis-ep-179
178. https://seekingalpha.com/article/4573494-fed-monopoly-money
179. https://www.amazon.com/Hasbro-A7444-Monopoly-Electronic-Banking/dp/B00EDBZ9F8
180. https://monopoly.fandom.com/wiki/Pirates_of_the_Caribbean_Collector%27s_Edition

A Financial Crisis to Usher in the Great Reset

Why did Silicon Valley Bank (SVB) fail?[181] This was a darling of the tech crowd.[182] They gave lavish amounts to progressive causes and liberal politicians.[183] Yet they were forced to close their doors following a bank run in early 2023. Why?

The truth is that reality showed up. This bank and many others were wildly profitable when rates were low, lending to speculators while paying depositors very little. They also bought lots of government bonds, pleasing the regulators. After all, what is safer than a U.S. Treasury bond? But what happens to the value of bonds, even good ones, when interest rates start to rise? Higher rates mean lower bond prices.[184] That's the law of the financial jungle. And Silicon Valley Bank (as did many others) had lots of those suddenly less-valuable bonds on their books.

When investors did the math, and marked their value to market, SVB no longer looked very good.[185] There was, in essence, a run on the bank where depositors began to pull money out. The FDIC stepped in, closed the bank, and made depositors whole. In a matter of days, other banks faced a similar fate.[186] The government had to step in to restore confidence.

Is that the last of it? A few banks gone, but everything else, OK? Hardly. Interest rates haven't gone back down. Sure, inflation has slowed but remains sticky. The Federal Reserve is caught in a trap. If

181. https://globaleconomicwarfare.com/2023/03/for-those-worried-about-the-silicon-valley-bank-failure/
182. https://kingsbusinessreview.co.uk/from-startup-darling-to-bank-failure-the-story-of-silicon-valley-bank
183. https://nypost.com/2023/03/15/svb-donated-73m-to-black-lives-matter-movement-social-justice-causes/
184. https://www.pimco.com/en-us/marketintelligence/navigating-interest-rates/how-do-rates-affect-bond-performance
185. https://www.npr.org/2023/03/19/1164531413/bank-fail-how-government-bonds-turned-toxic-for-silicon-valley-bank
186. https://www.fdic.gov/bank/historical/bank/bfb2023.html

they lower rates, inflation roars back. If they keep them high, we are on a path to bankruptcy from ever-growing interest payments and the banking system teeters on the edge of collapse.

My friend John Mauldin summed this up in his recent *Thoughts from the Frontline* (June 23, 2023):

> *We are running a $1.6 trillion deficit, which is slightly more than 6% of GDP. The government's interest expense is over $600 billion annually, even though a good portion was financed at lower rates. As those bonds roll off and we have to finance at higher rates, not to mention increasing the debt at a rate that will double it in just over 10 years, interest is going to consume the budget. That is one of the triggers for what I call The Great Reset.*[187]

Funny thing to note. John was talking about a Great Reset well before the World Economic Forum coopted the term.[188] He knew the board would have to be flipped at some point and debt would have to be dealt with. But Klaus Schwab (aka Dr. Evil) views this as an opportunity to remake the world in his vision and that of his cronies. It's a power grab, designed to use pain and fear to create a "New World Order," where you own nothing but are somehow going to be happy.[189] Sounds impossible now but after the fear and pain of a financial crisis, you may think differently.

Another Conspiracy Theory?

Like frogs in a kettle, we've let the temperature rise go unnoticed. But the water is about to boil. Don't let "normalcy bias" keep you from recognizing the truth. This is no conspiracy theory. It's hiding in plain sight. So much so that they outlined the goal in a November

187. https://www.mauldineconomics.com/frontlinethoughts/a-funny-kind-of-recession
188. https://www.mauldineconomics.com/frontlinethoughts/the-great-reset-vs.-the-great-reset
189. https://medium.com/yardcouch-com/you-will-own-nothing-and-be-happy-now-great-reset-2cb6ec88c732

2016 *Forbes* article written by Ida Auken (Young Global Leader and Member of the Global Future Council on Cities and Urbanization) for the World Economic Forum. The title? "Welcome To 2030: I Own Nothing, Have No Privacy and Life Has Never Been Better."[190] Here are some excerpts:

> *Welcome to the year 2030. Welcome to my city - or should I say, "our city." I don't own anything. I don't own a car. I don't own a house. I don't own any appliances or any clothes.*
>
> *It might seem odd to you, but it makes perfect sense for us in this city. Everything you considered a product, has now become a service. We have access to transportation, accommodation, food and all the things we need in our daily lives. One by one all these things became free, so it ended up not making sense for us to own much…*
>
> *Sometimes I use my bike when I go to see some of my friends. I enjoy the exercise and the ride. It kind of gets the soul to come along on the journey. Funny how some things seem never seem to lose their excitement: walking, biking, cooking, drawing and growing plants. It makes perfect sense and reminds us of how our culture emerged out of a close relationship with nature.*
>
> *In our city we don't pay any rent, because someone else is using our free space whenever we do not need it. My living room is used for business meetings when I am not there.*
>
> *Once in a while, I will choose to cook for myself. It is easy - the necessary kitchen equipment is delivered at my door within minutes. Since transport became free, we stopped having all those things stuffed into our home. Why keep a pasta-maker and a crepe cooker crammed into our cupboards? We can just order them when we need them.*

190. https://www.forbes.com/sites/worldeconomicforum/2016/11/10/shopping-i-cant-really-remember-what-that-is-or-how-differently-well-live-in-2030/

This also made the breakthrough of the circular economy easier. When products are turned into services, no one has an interest in things with a short life span. Everything is designed for durability, repairability and recyclability. The materials are flowing more quickly in our economy and can be transformed to new products pretty easily…

Shopping? I can't really remember what that is. For most of us, it has been turned into choosing things to use. Sometimes I find this fun, and sometimes I just want the algorithm to do it for me. It knows my taste better than I do by now.

When AI and robots took over so much of our work, we suddenly had time to eat well, sleep well and spend time with other people. The concept of rush hour makes no sense anymore, since the work that we do can be done at any time. I don't really know if I would call it work anymore. It is more like thinking-time, creation-time and development-time…

My biggest concern is all the people who do not live in our city. Those we lost on the way. Those who decided that it became too much, all this technology. Those who felt obsolete and useless when robots and AI took over big parts of our jobs. Those who got upset with the political system and turned against it. They live different kind of lives outside of the city. Some have formed little self-supplying communities. Others just stayed in the empty and abandoned houses in small 19th century villages.

Once in a while I get annoyed about the fact that I have no real privacy. Nowhere I can go and not be registered. I know that, somewhere, everything I do, think and dream of is recorded. I just hope that nobody will use it against me…

Of course, that writeup is just part of the equation. In this "utopia," you do what you are told, think as you are told, and have no money.

Why would you need it? Everything is free and all but the most minor decisions are made for you.

Are resources limitless? Is that how everything can be provided free? Of course not! Resources, goods, food, health care, energy are all scarce at any given time. That immutable reality can't be changed with a board flip. In fact, there will be fewer available resources if the free-market incentive to build, grow, develop, and maximize were removed. History has proven that. Even if you ignore that, building solar panels for green energy means you have less stuff to build other things like robots to do the work. Or to grow food. Even a simple life requires an ample supply and proper allocation of resources.

The truth is that these resources would be allocated first to the elites with what's left over divided up among the rest of us. History shows that also. Without money, you will have no say in any of it. Everyone will be impoverished while the Pigs run things, just like in George Orwell's classic, *Animal Farm*.[191] I made this point in detail in my book *According to Plan; The Elites' Secret Plan to Sabotage America*.[192]

The elites plan to silence you, ostracize you, and punish you unless you go along. We see that already in their ESG and DEI mandates. You must "toe the line" in regard to the Climate agenda, the race agenda, the gender agenda, and everything else. And they will be watching your every move, listening in at all times, just like the WEF writeup in Forbes explained:

> ***Once in a while I get annoyed about the fact that I have no real privacy. Nowhere I can go and not be registered. I know that, somewhere, everything I do, think and dream of is recorded. I just hope that nobody will use it against me.***

191. https://www.amazon.com/Animal-Farm-George-Orwell/dp/0451526341
192. https://www.amazon.com/dp/1958945005/

That's putting a spin on it! Of course, everything you say or do will be used against you, empowered by Artificial Intelligence and a mass surveillance state. This is reminiscent of George Orwell's other great dystopian novel, *1984.*[193]

Then there is Aldous Huxley's science fiction novel *Brave New World.*[194] This has all the dystopian horror of *1984* and *Animal Farm* but adds recreational drugs, irresponsible sex of all types, and babies raised by society rather than parents. Somehow that seems all too realistic as well. Everyone works for the state, and no one owns anything. Gee, that's a lot like the essay Ida Auken wrote for the WEF.[195] Authors Huxley and Orwell used to argue over what the future would look like. Turns out, they were both right in many ways.[196]

Understanding Dr. Evil

Just to make certain you understand how murderous The Great Reset would be to your personal Liberty, let's run through a dozen of its promised "features."[197]

193. https://www.amazon.com/1984-Essential-Orwell-Classics/dp/6257120896/
194. https://www.amazon.com/Brave-New-World-Aldous-Huxley/dp/0060850523
195. https://www.forbes.com/sites/worldeconomicforum/2016/11/10/shopping-i-cant-really-remember-what-that-is-or-how-differently-well-live-in-2030/?sh=17e7c4e91735
196. https://globaleconomicwarfare.com/2022/03/choose-your-dystopia/
197. https://www.opendemocracy.net/en/oureconomy/conspiracy-theories-aside-there-something-fishy-about-great-reset/

1. *The elimination of your automobile (which means taking away your ability to escape).*[198,199]
2. *The elimination of personal home ownership (ending the American Dream and your hope for privacy).*[200]
3. *Net Zero emissions (which eliminates practically anything you might want to do while creating a money-making scheme for elite hypocrites).*[201,202,203]
4. *Changing your diet from meat to bugs (no, really, that's the plan).*[204,205,206]
5. *Enforcing 15-minute cities (which become basically large prisons).*[207,208]
6. *Rationing health care as needed (need being defined by the state).*[209,210]
7. *Mandatory vaccines (and vaccine passports).*[211,212,213]
8. *Rationing water and limiting consumption.*[214]

198. https://www.foxbusiness.com/economy/world-economic-forum-calls-reduce-private-vehicles-by-eliminating-ownership
199. https://www.wsj.com/articles/world-economic-forum-paper-reduce-cars-by-2050-davos-private-jets-climate-f0bb64b9
200. https://mises.org/wire/no-privacy-no-property-world-2030-according-wef
201. https://www.weforum.org/projects/sustainable-banking
202. https://dailycaller.com/2023/05/06/opinion-the-great-carbon-capture-scam-jason-isaac/
203. https://nypost.com/2023/01/17/greenpeace-slams-billionaires-over-jet-hypocrisy-at-davos/
204. https://www.foxnews.com/media/davos-speaker-one-billion-people-stop-eating-meat-innovation-environment
205. https://www.foxnews.com/media/davos-speaker-one-billion-people-stop-eating-meat-innovation-environment
206. https://www.weforum.org/agenda/2022/02/how-insects-positively-impact-climate-change/
207. https://www.westernstandard.news/opinion/morgan-the-wefs-latest-push-is-the-15-minute-city/article_4a24b542-a7da-11ed-b1c2-e3aeed62aa09.html
208. https://www.theepochtimes.com/15-minute-cities-are-complete-impoverishment-and-enslavement-of-all-the-people_5231593.html
209. https://www3.weforum.org/docs/WEF_Insight_Report_Value_Healthcare_Laying_Foundation.pdf
210. https://www.reuters.com/article/us-healthcare-europe-systems-sb/factbox-europes-major-health-systems-and-how-they-work-idUSTRE57I2JQ20090819
211. https://www.facebook.com/worldeconomicforum/posts/if-we-dont-vaccinate-the-whole-world-as-we-should-covid-19-will-come-back-to-hau/10158144651456479/
212. https://www.weforum.org/agenda/2022/01/are-covid-19-vaccine-mandates-a-human-rights-violation/
213. https://www.weforum.org/videos/common-pass-travelling-the-world-in-the-covid-era
214. https://torontocaribbean.com/the-wef-have-big-plans-which-includes-rationing-the-water-humans-consume-what-is-next/

9. *Reducing the population to "sustainable levels" (dignified deaths for the weak, very few babies).*[215,216,217,218]
10. *Children raised (indoctrinated) by the state.*[219]
11. *A new religion and new bible written by artificial intelligence (while banning Christianity, Judaism, and if needed Islam).*[220]
12. *Eliminate capitalism and replace it with something to benefit all stakeholders.*[221,222,223,224]
13. *Rewrite history to make everything we know and love to be evil.*[225,226]

Sounds fun, doesn't it! Sadly, everything just listed (and more) is on the agenda.

How Do We Stop The Great Reset?

Here is the most important point of the chapter. Yes, there is a coming economic storm. Yes, the World Economic Forum and elitists plan to use the crisis to grab control. But they will need MONEY to do it. When they flip the game board, they will attempt to grab total control of money and we must not let them do it.

215. https://slaynews.com/news/wef-member-calls-86-reduction-worlds-population/
216. https://ourworld.unu.edu/en/dennis-meadows-limiting-growth-to-save-the-world
217. https://www.weforum.org/agenda/2009/01/live-and-let-die/
218. https://www.weforum.org/agenda/2018/04/almost-everywhere-people-are-having-fewer-children-so-do-we-still-need-to-worry-about-overpopulation/
219. https://www.usatoday.com/story/opinion/columnist/2023/04/27/biden-government-dictate-kids-education-schools-not-parents/11743676002/
220. https://www2.cbn.com/news/world/world-economic-forum-contributor-says-ai-could-rewrite-bible-create-correct-religions
221. https://www.weforum.org/agenda/2020/07/to-build-back-better-we-must-reinvent-capitalism-heres-how/
222. https://www.nationalreview.com/2021/08/stakeholder-capitalism-a-sham-unfortunately-not/
223. https://wokecapital.org/what-really-is-esg/
224. https://www.washingtonexaminer.com/politics/revolt-of-the-fat-cats
225. https://xotv.me/channels/233-economic-war-room/vod_videos/9917-the-marxist-deception-about-our-founding-fathers-and-america-guests-david-and-tim-barton-ep-152
226. https://xotv.me/channels/233-economic-war-room/vod_videos/4947-howard-zinns-distorted-view-of-american-history-and-his-dangerous-impact-on-america-with-guest-mary-grabar-ep-83

That's right. It comes back to money because money is either freedom or slavery as we have shown. That is good news. They already have the politicians, the education system, the governments, bureaucracies, and even the corporations. But they don't have full control of the money, at least not yet.

Now, I have to admit they've done a pretty good job of controlling much of the money in the world through investments, ESG mandates, and Index Funds like Blackrock, State Street, and Vanguard. That is despite the fact that the founder of the Index Fund industry, Jack Bogle, warned us shortly before his death.[227] Yes, these groups have captured tens of trillions of dollars under management.[228] But the pushback has started and the pushback is succeeding as people become aware.[229,230]

We've been doing our part in the Economic War Room and by training financial advisors at the NSIC Institute (via Liberty University).[231,232] And we work with some amazing groups like National Center's Free Enterprise Project,[233] Consumer's Research, State Financial Officers Foundation,[234] Capital Research Center,[235] the Political Forum,[236] 1792 Exchange,[237] as well as non-woke asset managers like Strive,[238]

227. https://www.wsj.com/articles/bogle-sounds-a-warning-on-index-funds-1543504551
228. https://www.bloomberg.com/professional/blog/esg-assets-may-hit-53-trillion-by-2025-a-third-of-global-aum/
229. https://www.heritage.org/environment/heritage-explains/the-esg-pushback
230. https://www.washingtonexaminer.com/restoring-america/courage-strength-optimism/conservatives-are-winning-the-war-against-esg
231. https://www.economicwarroom.com/
232. https://www.nsic.org/
233. https://xotv.me/channels/233-economic-war-room/vod_videos/15680-the-woke-incentive-its-all-about-the-money-or-is-it-guest-scott-shepard-ep-246
234. https://xotv.me/channels/233-economic-war-room/vod_videos/15143-holding-state-governors-and-legislators-accountable-when-they-dont-act-in-the-publics-financial-interests-guest-derek-kreifels-ep-215
235. https://xotv.me/channels/233-economic-war-room/vod_videos/4979-blm-funding-its-time-to-follow-the-money-with-guest-scott-walter-ep-99
236. https://xotv.me/channels/233-economic-war-room/vod_videos/6821-woke-capital-and-political-correctness-have-captured-big-business-guest-stephen-soukup-ep-129
237. https://xotv.me/channels/233-economic-war-room/vod_videos/15552-game-changing-investment-tool-that-exposes-woke-companies-guest-paul-fitzpatrick-ep-233
238. https://rumble.com/v2q07oj-the-new-global-monarchy-the-big-3-mega-fund-ceos-guest-justin-danhof-ep-243.html

Amberwave Partners,[239] Point Bridge Capital,[240] Alpha Investor,[241] and Timothy Plan[242,243] (a proud sponsor of Economic War Room). The fact is that when people are educated about ESG, they reject it and pull back their investments.[244] That's a great start.

Monetary policy is the larger play for unlimited money. When the game board gets flipped, we know the plan is to introduce CBDC. They have to. And this is where we must stop them.

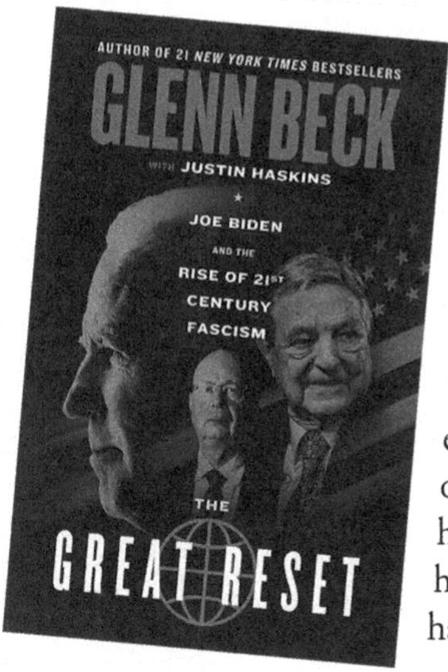

Glenn Beck and Justin Haskins wrote a terrific book, *The Great Reset, Joe Biden and the Rise of 21st Century Fascism*.[245] I interviewed Glenn when it came out and offered the one "gold bullet" that would stop it. You know how silver bullets kill werewolves? Well, I explained the gold bullet that could end the Great Reset. I love the look on Glenn's face when I shared it with him.[246] He instantly understood because he knows that the Great Reset does not happen without total monetary control.

239. https://xotv.me/channels/233-economic-war-room/vod_videos/14926-former-treasury-official-offers-unique-solution-to-woke-wall-street-guest-tom-dans-ep-207
240. https://xotv.me/channels/233-economic-war-room/vod_videos/15043-an-alternative-to-woke-esg-investing-guest-hal-lambert-ep-210
241. https://xotv.me/channels/233-economic-war-room/vod_videos/13111-why-woke-investing-will-ultimately-fail-guest-charles-mizrahi-ep-164
242. https://xotv.me/channels/233-economic-war-room/vod_videos/7201-a-new-approach-to-the-woke-company-profit-problem-ep-134
243. https://xotv.me/channels/233-economic-war-room/vod_videos/4913-68-percent-of-mutual-fund-wealth-is-owned-by-christians-so-what-economic-war-room-ep-67
244. https://d3n8a8pro7vhmx.cloudfront.net/economicwarroom/pages/786/attachments/original/1601992402/ep108_Economic_Battle_Plan™_John_McLaughlin.pdf
245. https://www.glennbeck.com/glenns-books/the-great-reset
246. https://xotv.me/channels/233-economic-war-room/vod_videos/13871-the-great-reset-and-real-solutions-to-stop-it-now-guest-glenn-beck-ep-176 (watch the 3rd segment starting at -5:24)

In Chapter 4 ("Modern Monetary Theory: Fuel for a Global Economic Takeover," page 149), Glenn writes:

> *The Great Reset is a machine manufactured to usher in a new, highly sophisticated, technologically advanced, twenty-first century brand of international fascism, one with a corporate twist.* ***But powerful machines like the Great Reset cannot operate without fuel.*** *That is what modern monetary theory provides, by offering seemingly endless amounts of money that could be used to pay for just about anything government, corporations, and financial institutions can dream up.*

We now know that the existing monetary structure will be upended, to be replaced by CBDC. The Great Reset folks have to have programmable money. It's how they plan to control people and the economy, expanding the money supply at a whim and cutting it off as needed to achieve their objective. If CBDC (aka Biden Bucks) is the only alternative, they win. That is why it is so imperative that we produce a credible alternative.

In World War II, the Battle of the Bulge marked an unbelievable Nazi offensive that almost reversed the outcome of the war in late 1944.[247] More than 200,000 German troops and 1,000 Panzer tanks struck the Allies just before Christmas. They rapidly advanced against the Americans who were complacent, assuming the war was already won. There's a wonderful movie about this starring Henry Fonda and Robert Shaw.[248] In it, Fonda's character, Lt. Colonel Kiley, serves as an Army intelligence officer who uncovers the German weakness. They have powerful tanks but lack a steady supply of fuel. His character survives a plane crash and manages to blow up the Allied fuel depot, essentially running the Panzers out of gas. The ending scene is a miles-long line of disheartened German troops walking

247. https://www.army.mil/botb/
248. https://www.imdb.com/title/tt0058947/

home in defeat. The movie told that story accurately.[249] Great war machines require fuel and without it they fail.

The Great Reset cannot occur without an unlimited supply of money and CBDC is their only potential source. The existing dollar-based framework is about to fail (as we've shown). And even if it doesn't implode on its own, our enemies are planning to take it down as we will explain in Chapter Five.

BUT…. If we can provide a credible, Constitutional, convenient, safe, and useful legal-tender alternative, people will flock to it. There's a saying on Wall Street that "money goes where it is treated best." **State-based, transactional modern pirate money (gold and silver) is the answer! It is the Gold (and Silver) Bullet to stop the Great Reset.**

249. https://390th.org/nazi-germanys-quest-for-oil-and-the-battle-of-the-bulge/

KEVIN AND HIS RUSSIAN MONOPOLY GAME.

How the mighty have fallen, and the weapons of war perished!
—2 Samuel 1:27 (NKJV)

5

BEWARE THE DRAGON

We've just outlined how our own government, colluding with Dr. Evil and the World Economic Forum, plan to enslave you with your own money following a massive economic crisis. That's bad enough, right? Unfortunately, that's only half of the threat equation. Don't you wish you could borrow a time machine and go back to the simple days of Five and Dime stores, fifteen-cent comics, and quarter Slurpees? I sure do.

Unfortunately, we are in the 2020s living without the flying cars and hoverboards we were promised. [We are told they are still being tested but "coming soon."[250,251,252]] In the introduction, I shared that inflation was just one of the threats to your future. Now we have CBDC and the Great Reset. But wait . . . there's more. Seems like a nightmare version of an informercial. Instead of getting a free set of

250. https://nypost.com/2020/08/28/japans-flying-car-soars-in-test-flight-with-person-aboard/
251. https://slate.com/technology/2012/11/wheres-my-hoverboard-sorry-youre-probably-never-getting-one.html
252. https://www.zmescience.com/feature-post/technology-articles/inventions-1/hoverboards-real-science-07112021/

Ginsu knives or an extra drying rack for your new food dehydrator, there's another bonus calamity coming your way. The current global "hot mess" is getting more challenging by the day…war over Ukraine, threats to Taiwan, pandemics with tin-pot dictators forcing lockdowns, masks, and vaccine passports.

It really wasn't that long ago when the world seemed . . . well better. In 2019, just before the pandemic, our economy was humming.[253] Sure, we were still on a bad debt trajectory, but there was at least the potential to alter course (that is, before we added another $10 trillion in "pandemic relief" over three years).[254,255] But in 2019, the United States finally was standing up to the unfair trade practices of China, reasserting our leadership in the global economy.[256] Then, people started getting ill. We now know the virus likely came from a lab in Wuhan (after being told it was racist to consider that).[257,258,259] We also know that the Chinese Communist Party caused it to be exported around the world through travel policy.[260] And that they hoarded the personal protection equipment (PPE) the world would need.[261] But before that, in 2019, things seemed more hopeful.

Looking further back, maybe 30 years, things looked even brighter. We had beaten communism (or so we imagined) with the collapse of the Soviet Union and the fall of the Berlin Wall. America was the clear technology leader of the world with smartphones and the

253. https://trumpwhitehouse.archives.gov/articles/united-states-gdp-growth-continues-exceeding-expectations/
254. https://www.mckinsey.com/industries/public-sector/our-insights/the-10-trillion-dollar-rescue-how-governments-can-deliver-impact
255. https://www.theatlantic.com/ideas/archive/2020/05/we-can-prevent-a-great-depression-itll-take-10-trillion/611749/
256. https://trumpwhitehouse.archives.gov/briefings-statements/president-donald-j-trump-confronting-chinas-unfair-trade-policies/
257. https://www.marshall.senate.gov/newsroom/press-releases/wall-street-journal-exclusive-u-s-funded-scientist-who-worked-at-wuhan-lab-one-of-the-first-presumptive-positive-cases/
258. https://www.amazon.com/CCP-War-America-Communist-Biological/dp/B0B592KTZG/
259. https://www.nationalreview.com/2021/06/the-lab-leak-theory-is-unbearably-racist/
260. https://economictimes.indiatimes.com/blogs/Whathappensif/how-china-locked-down-internally-for-covid-19-but-pushed-foreign-travel/
261. https://www.forbes.com/sites/isabeltogoh/2020/05/04/china-covered-up-coronavirus-to-hoard-medical-supplies-dhs-report-finds/?sh=97179691dbab

Internet soon to change the planet. Global free markets were the rage. American military power displaced Saddam Hussein (and the 4th largest army on the planet) from Kuwait in a literal 100 hours.[262] Gone was the stench of defeat from Vietnam. Seinfeld made TV funny again. The future looked absolutely incredible for America. Then came 9/11, a financial crisis, and later the pandemic.

Now, we are facing the demise of our currency with the threat of being bankrupted like Argentina, Venezuela, Zimbabwe, Greece, and Weimar Germany before us.

So how did we get where we are now when things once looked so good? A lot of what we face properly can be attributed to our own malfeasance, greed, and avarice. That's on us. But there's more to it than that, as explained by two Chinese senior PLA (Peoples Liberation Army) colonels in what may be the most important book you probably never heard of. *Unrestricted Warfare* was published in 1999. The subtitle (added by later editors) is *China's Master Plan to Destroy America.*[263,264] I remember carrying a copy into the Pentagon back in 2009, shocking Admirals and Generals. I showed my copy to a former CIA Director who almost couldn't believe it was real. Back then, the top brass all insisted that China was our ally, friend, banker, and favorite trading partner. "They love America," I was told, and "would never harm us." My message of economic warfare and the truth of Chinese *Unrestricted Warfare* were largely ignored and sometimes denounced.[265]

262. https://history.army.mil/html/bookshelves/resmat/desert-storm/index.html
263. https://www.amazon.com/Unrestricted-Warfare-Chinas-Destroy-America/dp/1626543054
264. https://www.c4i.org/unrestricted.pdf
265. https://www.washingtontimes.com/news/2011/feb/28/financial-terrorism-suspected-in-08-economic-crash/

In hindsight, it should be obvious that *Unrestricted Warfare* was and remains a war plan being waged against America. The book's preface makes it clear that the Chinese communists were deathly fearful of a strong America and prepared to do whatever necessary to tear us down. They knew our military was vastly superior, having witnessed how easily we removed an entrenched Iraq from Kuwait a few years earlier. At the time, the Chinese economy was an afterthought in the world, roughly one-tenth the size of America and on par with Italy (based on nominal GDP).[266] Hard to imagine, but that was the reality just a couple decades ago. In the shortest time possible, China went from third-world country to global superpower. How?

The answer is *Unrestricted Warfare*. Whether biological warfare, resources warfare, coopting (bribing) foreign officials, regulatory warfare, intellectual property theft, media warfare, or financial warfare (and so much more), the PLA explained it in the book and then carried it out in action. Interestingly, the authors were fascinated with two individuals that they described as the future of warfare. The first was Osama Bin Laden. The second, George Soros.

> *For bin Laden who hides under the hills of Islamic fundamentalism, Soros who conceals himself within the forests of free economics, and the computer hackers who hide themselves in the green curtains of networks, no national boundaries exist, and borders also are ineffective. What they want to do is carry out wanton destruction within a regulated sphere and act wildly and run amuck within an unregulated sphere. These new terrorist forces have formed an unprecedented serious challenge to the existing world order…*[267]

> *If…bin Laden, and Soros can be considered soldiers in the wars of tomorrow, then who isn't a soldier?*[268]

266. https://knoema.com/mhrzolg/historical-gdp-by-country-statistics-from-the-world-bank-1960-2019
267. https://www.c4i.org/unrestricted.pdf page 136
268. Ibid, page 222

Amazingly, this was written almost three years before 9/11. Before anyone other than a few intelligence analysts had even heard of Osama bin Laden. Some have suggested the Chinese Communists were friendly with al Qaeda in the late 1990s.[269] What is obvious is that they were admirers of his disruptive warfare potential. They recognized that an attack on our World Trade Center would cost very little to carry out yet would wreak havoc and cost America trillions of dollars in response.[270]

> *Whether it be the intrusions of hackers, a major explosion at the World Trade Center, or a bombing attack by bin Laden, all of these greatly exceed the frequency band widths understood by the American military.*[271]

One estimate of the total cost of our war on terror has been $21 trillion, accounting for two-thirds of our current debt predicament.[272] If that's not economic warfare, what is?

The second "hero" mentioned was George Soros, whom the Chinese authors ultimately likened to a financial terrorist.

> *We believe that before long, "financial warfare" will undoubtedly be an entry in the various types of dictionaries of official military jargon. Moreover, when people revise the history books on twentieth-century warfare in the early 21st century, the section on financial warfare will command the reader's utmost attention. The main protagonist in this section of the history book will not be a statesman or a military strategist; rather, it will be George Soros.*[273]

269. https://www.hudson.org/national-security-defense/the-historical-evolution-of-al-qaeda-s-positions-on-china
270. https://foreignpolicy.com/2010/11/23/death-by-a-thousand-cuts-2/
271. https://www.c4i.org/unrestricted.pdf pages 144-45
272. https://www.newsweek.com/war-terror-cost-us-21-trillion-its-conflicts-killed-nearly-one-million-reports-show-1625114
273. https://www.c4i.org/unrestricted.pdf page 52

What earned Soros such respect? No doubt the authors understood exactly what he did when he "broke the Bank of England" by assaulting the British pound in 1992.[274] And his methods became their primary choice of weapon to ultimately beat America.

> *To stir up the waters and grope for fish, the likes of Soros combine speculation in currency markets, stock markets, and futures markets. Also, they exploit public opinion and create widespread momentum to lure and assemble the "jumbos" … to join forces in the marketplace on a huge scale and wage hair-raising financial wars one after the other.*[275]

Bottom Line? The Chinese warfare strategy became to displace if not destroy the American dollar. Bin Laden had done his part, setting in motion a typically American response of throwing trillions of dollars into a War on Terror. Now it was time for the Soros plan. In 2010, in an official house organ of the Chinese Communist Party (Qiushi magazine), their strategy was outlined.[276,277]

> *Of course, to fight the U.S., we have to come up with key "weapons." What is the most powerful weapon China has today? It is our economic power, especially our foreign exchange reserves. The key is to use it well. If we use it well, it is a weapon; otherwise it may become a burden. Counting on the fact that the U.S. dollar is the international currency, the U.S. government has increased the number of dollars in circulation, leading to its devaluation…*
>
> *If no one purchases them, then they will only be circulated domestically, inside the U.S., and cause inflation. In order for the countries with foreign exchange reserves in the U.S. dollar to restrain the U.S. from over-issuing U.S. currency, they must act together and not buy U.S. dollars…*

274. https://www.thebalancemoney.com/black-wednesday-george-soros-bet-against-britain-1978944
275. https://www.c4i.org/unrestricted.pdf page 194
276. http://chinascope.org/wp-content/uploads/2011/02/R20101213A_GoogleCache.pdf
277. https://globaleconomicwarfare.com/2013/10/dont-miss-the-chinese-warning-the-dollar-is-at-risk/

> *The fact that the U.S. dollar is the world's reserve currency makes the U.S. a financial superpower. Currently, China's increased share in the International Monetary Fund and its increased voting rights are a very big step forward. The problem is not that the value of this share is expressed in U.S. dollars, but that it would be best if the share could be expressed in RMB. Therefore, for China to challenge the position of the U.S. dollar, it needs to take a path of internationalization and directly confront the U.S. dollar.*

The article goes on to discuss forming an anti-dollar alliance including India and Saudi Arabia with China taking the lead. This in many ways was the genesis of the anti-dollar BRICS now forming. Putin's Russia was already against the dollar.[278,279] They just needed to convince Brazil and later South Africa, and Saudi Arabia, to ultimately create a 30-nation alliance (now coming into place) and destroy the American dollar.[280,281,282]

This is not new. It is simply accelerating.[283] And our profligate spending has made it easy for them. Shortly after Xi Jinping took power, China called for "de-Americanizing" the planet by destroying our currency.[284] China apologists in Washington were quick to claim, "he didn't mean it." You know, the same voices who later said that it's racist to claim that Covid escaped from a Chinese lab.[285] Of course, history has proven that president-for-life (dictator) Xi did, in fact, mean what he said. It was and remains official Chinese policy to destroy our currency and de-Americanize the world.

278. https://globaleconomicwarfare.com/2013/02/putin-prepares-for-a-currency-war-that-he-thinks-hopes-will-collapse-america/
279. https://globaleconomicwarfare.com/2014/07/voice-of-russia-brics-morphing-into-anti-dollar-alliance/
280. https://watcher.guru/news/brics-30-countries-ditch-u-s-dollar-as-global-reserve-currency
281. https://dailyhodl-com.cdn.ampproject.org/c/s/dailyhodl.com/2023/04/28/24-nations-align-against-us-dollar-as-brics-looks-to-launch-new-global-currency/amp/
282. https://www.cryptopolitan.com/syria-joins-trend-ditches-us-dollar-for-yuan/
283. https://www.newarab.com/analysis/gulf-states-and-de-dollarisation-trend
284. https://www.ibtimes.co.uk/china-debt-ceiling-shutdown-xinhua-de-emericanised-513431
285. https://www.washingtonpost.com/news/worldviews/wp/2013/10/14/calm-down-washington-china-doesnt-really-want-to-de-americanize/

It is worth noting that in 2008, China held as much as 17% of America's outstanding debt ($1.7 trillion out of $10 trillion).[286] Today, their holdings are less than 3% ($859 billion out of $32 trillion).[287] In other words, they have been putting their money where their mouth is. Literally.

How has China Turned the World Against Us?

As in most of our current challenges, our arrogance gives China the opportunity. I call it "the myth of dollar permanence."[288] We have assumed that our printed (paper/fiat Federal Reserve note) dollar bills are the only real money, desired by everyone, anywhere in the world for all times. That may have been true once but is no longer the case. And yet, we continue in arrogance, using our money as a weapon, ignoring the very real cost of the largest debt by any nation in the history of the world.[289] We have viewed our creditors as being subject to our needs rather than the normal other way around. And we have used the dollar in sanctions to manipulate and control the behavior of other sovereign nations.[290]

When I served as a contracted Economic Warfare consultant to the DoD, I was careful to warn that the dollar was at risk if we didn't address our debts and deficits. In fact, I went further. As early as 2008, I laid out the intention for a Phase 3 attack to ruin America for good. Phase 1 was a manipulation of the energy markets. Phase 2 was an attack on our banking system. Phase 3 was a direct assault on the dollar itself.[291] We are now in Phase 3.

Beyond that, I, along with others, warned that the constant use of sanctions would discourage other nations, even allies from holding

286. https://www.cfr.org/blog/who-bought-all-treasuries-us-issued-2008-and-who-will-be-big-buyers-2009
287. https://usafacts.org/articles/which-countries-own-the-most-us-debt/
288. https://globaleconomicwarfare.com/2012/11/the-myth-of-dollar-permanence/
289. https://asiatimes.com/2023/06/world-economy-changing-americans-know-but-their-leaders-dont/
290. https://dailyreckoning.com/rickards-were-our-own-worst-enemy/
291. https://www.scribd.com/document/49755779/Economic-Warfare-Risks-and-Responses-by-Kevin-D-Freeman

dollars.[292,293] It only stands to reason that when other countries watch us punish Russia by preventing their use of American dollars, they wonder what would happen if they were to get on our bad side.[294] Then when they see America meddling in their internal affairs (like pushing gender policies they don't want), it becomes obvious they must get off dollars.[295,296]

Elon Musk made that clear when he tweeted:

> "If you weaponize currency enough times, other countries will stop using it."[297]

Many others agree.[298,299]

292. https://www.cnbc.com/2022/03/22/countries-may-want-to-diversify-away-from-the-us-dollar-think-tank.html
293. https://www.tasnimnews.com/en/news/2023/04/30/2887530/us-dollar-biggest-economic-terrorism-in-world-indian-banker-says
294. https://jacobin.com/2022/04/us-dollar-ukraine-war-global-dominance-currency-sanctions-russia
295. https://www.brookings.edu/blog/future-development/2023/03/02/the-biden-harris-administrations-gender-strategies-and-policies-strengths-challenges-and-opportunities/
296. https://mishtalk.com/economics/dollar-weaponization-expands-fdic-message-to-foreign-depositors-is-dont-trust-the-us/
297. https://twitter.com/elonmusk/status/1650741654066806784
298. https://markets.businessinsider.com/news/currencies/dedollarization-currencies-elon-musk-ray-dalio-chamath-palihapitiya-2023-5
299. https://dailyreckoning.com/rickards-drops-bombshell/

China comes calling with sweetheart deals, a Belt and Road Initiative, and economic support to help other nations abandon our currency.[300,301] Plus, you should know that China, Russia, and many other countries have been stockpiling gold.[302]

Fareed Zakaria (from CNN fame) wrote a column in *The Washington Post* with the title, *Opinion: The dollar is our superpower, and Russia and China are threatening it.* In it he said:

> *The dollar is America's superpower. It gives Washington unrivaled economic and political muscle. The United States can slap sanctions on countries unilaterally, freezing them out of large parts of the world economy. And when Washington spends freely, it can be certain that its debt, usually in the form of T-bills, will be bought up by the rest of the world.*
>
> *Sanctions imposed on Russia for its invasion of Ukraine combined with Washington's increasingly confrontational approach to China have created a perfect storm in which both Russia and China are accelerating efforts to diversify away from the dollar. Their central banks are keeping less of their reserves in dollars, and most trade between them is being settled in the yuan. They are also, as Putin noted, making efforts to get other countries to follow suit.*[303]

Strong and accurate statement. It just comes about 15 years late.

300. https://foreignpolicy.com/2022/09/21/china-yuan-us-dollar-sco-currency/
301. https://news.bitcoin.com/venezuela-to-integrate-russian-mir-payments-system-in-de-dollarization-push/
302. https://www.usgoldbureau.com/news/why-is-china-buying-so-much-gold
303. https://www.washingtonpost.com/opinions/2023/03/24/us-dollar-strength-russia-china/

Could the Dollar Really be Dethroned?

The last nation to officially lose reserve currency status was the UK sometime around World War II. The decline started shortly after the end of World War I and continued gradually through the first part of the 1950s according to *Financial Times*.[304] It wasn't sudden, and it wasn't vindictive. But the British clearly lost national power. In fact, they lost it so clearly that the United States was able to dictate their foreign policy in the Suez Canal incident of 1956. That is when Egypt unilaterally nationalized the Canal that the French built nearly a century before and had been operated by a joint venture owned by the British and French. When Egypt nationalized it in 1956, Britain, France, and Israel became concerned and began plans to retake it by force.

As the dethroned former reserve currency, the British were heavily in debt. The new powerhouse, America, owned a lot of UK bonds and controlled their access to capital. President Eisenhower used this leverage to stop any move to retake the Canal, humiliating Britain and demonstrating clearly that they were no longer a major player. And we did this to our most important ally. How much more would our enemies like to humiliate us if given the chance?

Here is an Army War College report on the incident:

> *With just three offensive strikes, the United States achieved its immediate policy aims of forcing Britain and then France to withdraw from the Suez Canal. The three financial warfare strikes were: (1) blocking the International Monetary Fund (IMF) from providing Britain with $561 million in standby credit; (2) blocking the US Export-Import Bank from extending $600 million in credit to Britain; and (3) threatening to dump America's holdings of pound-sterling bonds unless Great Britain withdrew from the Suez. The credit blockade froze Britain's ability to borrow and forced it back onto its negative*

304. https://www.ft.com/content/9ce54a9e-be11-4b61-bf49-f2cfe5b22628

cash flow, effectively bankrupting it. The pound-sterling threat significantly raised the perceived risk of dealing in British currency. That threat, if executed, would have directly affected British ability to trade internationally.

By 1956, Britain was grossly overleveraged and dependent on further international borrowing to maintain its standard of living. The United States owned $3.75 billion in British debt as a result of the Anglo-American Loan Agreement of 1945, while the entire foreign currency reserve of Britain in October 1956 was equivalent to $2.2 billion. To finance its WW II efforts, Britain had borrowed extensively from Commonwealth members and by 1945 owed roughly £14 billion, chiefly to India, Argentina, and Egypt. Unable to repay in full, Britain froze the principal balances in these accounts.

The sell-off of US-held pound-sterling bonds, if executed, would have been catastrophic. The resulting increase of British currency in circulation would have deflated the value of the pound-sterling. This deflation would, in turn, have required Britain to drain its foreign currency reserves to buy pound-sterling bonds to maintain its currency's parity against the US dollar. If it broke parity, and allowed the devaluation of its currency, Britain would not have the purchasing power or the foreign reserves to cover its food and energy imports... Without credit, Britain would have faced a prolonged liquidity crisis and insolvency.

This Suez Crisis example illustrates the importance of understanding the offensive capabilities and defensive necessities of financial warfare. ***The United States successfully waged financial warfare against the third most powerful nation on the planet at that time; it is likely the United States will be targeted by financial warfare in the future.***[305]

305. https://press.armywarcollege.edu/cgi/viewcontent.cgi?article=2956&context=parameters

Unfortunately, that was written a decade ago and the future is now.

Eisenhower's actions set the stage for Soros to take down the British pound a few years later. If we would do that to the British, don't you know China wants to do it to us? And they have built a coalition of 30+ nations ready to help them, many resenting how they have been treated by the United States over the years.[306] As a result, we are now watching de-dollarization play out before our eyes according to *Asia Times*.[307] And the official Chinese News Agency says the process is accelerating.

> *The question is about when, not if, the hegemony of the U.S. dollar will end, with more countries across the Global South seeking alternatives... As a result of Washington imposing sweeping sanctions on Moscow, freezing Russia's U.S. dollar reserves, and removing major Russian banks from SWIFT, de-dollarization has accelerated.*[308]

This warning was front and center in my Pentagon reports. In fact, here is a public excerpt that was published in a 2012 *American Legion Magazine* article with the title, "The Message No One Wanted to Hear":

> ***The Coming Third Phase***. *The third phase requires the loss of America's Triple-A credit rating (which happened last August) and ultimately the removal of the U.S. dollar as the world's primary reserve currency. This type of attack would put the United States in a similar position as Greece and Italy, mandating severe defense cuts and a major reduction of U.S. power around the planet.*
>
> *When my white-paper report on economic warfare was first presented in 2009, there was a good deal of pushback. The*

306. https://www.deccanherald.com/international/world-news-politics/brics-pitches-for-using-local-currencies-in-international-trade-1224179.html
307. https://asiatimes.com/2023/06/are-we-living-through-a-de-dollarization/
308. https://english.news.cn/europe/20230609/c7f03bcceba74ad3a023d93118e9b048/c.html

defense community said they didn't really understand the economics. The economists couldn't grasp why anyone would do this, since harming the U.S. economy would hurt other nations, especially China. Even as we saw the predicted third phase unfold before our eyes and even as China gained vis-à-vis the United States from the crisis, the pushback continued.

The Chinese colonels understood in 1999 that financial warfare would be difficult for Americans to grasp. They wrote:

"The Americans have not been able to get their act together in this area. This is because proposing a new concept of weapons does not rely on the springboard of new technology; it just demands lucid and incisive thinking. However, this is not a strong point of the Americans ..."[309]

Whether or not China can dethrone the dollar remains to be seen. But the Chinese are making progress and recently hit a milestone. The Chinese yuan just passed the dollar as the most used currency in China's cross-border transactions. That's the first time in modern history.[310] It's crazy not to recognize that China is already at war with us.[311,312] It's just an Unrestricted War.[313,314,315,316,317,318]

309. https://www.legion.org/magazine/162503/message-no-one-wanted-hear
310. https://wltreport.com/2023/04/26/china-overtakes-u-s-in-historic-first/
311. https://townhall.com/tipsheet/mattvespa/2023/05/02/everyone-is-preparing-for-war-between-china-and-the-united-states-n2622707
312. https://www.foreignaffairs.com/united-states/xi-jinping-says-he-preparing-china-war
313. https://globaleconomicwarfare.com/2011/06/is-china-at-war-with-the-usa/
314. https://www.reuters.com/world/china/with-eye-ukraine-top-chinese-general-calls-unconventional-warfare-capabilities-2023-05-16/
315. https://www.asiafinancial.com/chinese-general-urges-more-use-of-tech-financial-warfare
316. https://www.wionews.com/world/top-chinese-general-bats-for-building-up-hybrid-warfare-capabilities-592875
317. https://financialpost.com/pmn/business-pmn/with-eye-on-ukraine-top-chinese-general-calls-for-unconventional-warfare-capabilities
318. https://www.ntd.com/chinese-hackers-attack-on-key-us-bases-on-guam-is-part-of-unrestricted-warfare-military-expert_923196.html

How Would This Impact You?

This is the scary part. If we lose our reserve currency status, we will be formally bankrupt. Interest rates would skyrocket as the government initially desperately seeks capital to continue spending or even just to pay the interest on debt.[319] Eventually, if the dollar collapsed, the financial crisis would force one or more dire scenarios:

1. *The government might be forced to slash spending on everything, even the military. Social Security, Medicare, salaries, benefits, all could be on the chopping block. They'd try to hold as much as possible in place (especially keeping enough military to protect the government) but over time the capacity to spend money we don't have would be eliminated. This could set off a depression resulting in mass unemployment.*[320]

2. *The government could do a "taking." Under this scenario, the government confiscates the wealth it needs to continue operations. This could be done by tax policy, taxing bitcoin or gold to suck out the gains. Or it could be an outright confiscation as happened to gold under Roosevelt's 1933 Executive Order. Take the gold and set the price for it artificially low.*[321] *Beyond that, the government might do what other failed economies have done.*[322] *Force investors into government bonds "for their safety."*[323]

3. *The government could simply print money as needed. This is modern monetary theory and would result in hyperinflation.*[324]

319. https://www.investopedia.com/terms/s/sovereign-default.asp
320. https://www.cnbc.com/2013/10/03/first-a-default-then-a-depression-some-think-so.html
321. https://www.federalreservehistory.org/essays/gold-reserve-act
322. https://www.bloomberg.com/news/articles/2023-03-24/argentina-credit-rating-cut-by-fitch-on-public-sector-debt-swap#xj4y7vzkg
323. https://youtu.be/SrcqJE8HYf8
324. https://www.investopedia.com/terms/h/hyperinflation.asp

> *It happened in Zimbabwe.*[325] *It happened in Germany.*[326] *It happened in Hungary and Yugoslavia.*[327] *Most recently, it is happening in Venezuela and Argentina.*[328,329] *There have been more than 56 examples in modern times, each stemming from excessive money printing.*[330]

What would this feel like? Reuters recently explained the impact of hyperinflation in Argentina happening right now:

> *Argentina's annual inflation rate soared to 104.3% in March, the official statistics agency said on Friday, one of the highest rates in the world, straining people's wallets and stoking a cost-of-living crisis that has pushed up poverty.*
>
> *The inflation reading for the month came in at 7.7%, well above analyst forecasts of 7.1%, marking the fastest monthly rise since 2002 and piling pressure on the government…*

325. https://river.com/learn/history-of-monetary-collapse-in-zimbabwe
326. https://www.smithsonianmag.com/history/how-hyperinflation-heralded-the-fall-of-german-democracy-180982204/
327. https://www.investopedia.com/articles/personal-finance/122915/worst-hyperinflations-history.asp
328. https://www.reuters.com/world/americas/venezuela-inflation-accelerating-heightening-risk-return-hyperinflation-2023-01-05/
329. https://www.reuters.com/world/americas/zero-capacity-save-argentines-buckle-under-103-inflation-2023-04-14/
330. https://www.cato.org/working-paper/world-hyperinflations

> *"I try to think that someday we're going to be better off. But the inflation we're living with today in Argentina is terrible. It feels like never before," said Claudia Hernansaez, a publishing company employee. "In my case, I have zero capacity to save." The soaring prices have hammered salaries and spending power, pushed up poverty to near 40%..."We know, it hurts us, it occupies us, how this affects daily life and every family," she added, saying the government hoped a downward trend in inflation would be "reflected soon."*
>
> *For now, every trip to the supermarket is a reminder of the country's inflationary crisis, the worst since 1991, which was the end of a period of hyperinflation. Retiree Juan Tartara said prices spiked with each weekly visit to the store. "Sometimes food increases 10% or 15%," he said. "In one year, beef went from around 1,000 pesos ($4.66) or 1,200 pesos to 2,800 pesos."*
>
> *Paola Lavezzari, also in publishing, said inflation was forcing her to tighten the purse strings and buy cheaper products. "The first thing you lose is the quality of the product. Because what you used to consume of a better quality, today is unaffordable," she said. "Things were always maybe 10 pesos more, but now it's 100 pesos more. ... When you make the monthly shopping trip, it's so much. The difference is huge."*[331]

The sad thing is that compared to many hyperinflations, the Argentine experience has so far been mild, as devastating as it must be. The bottom line is that in hyperinflation your quality of life would suffer. A lot. Worse things could happen as well, such as a collapse in our government or even an invasion through porous borders. One Russian academic predicted that America would disintegrate into six separate zones. Why? He said the "pyramid scheme" of U.S. debt would collapse "and predicted China and Russia would usurp

331. https://www.reuters.com/world/americas/zero-capacity-save-argentines-buckle-under-103-inflation-2023-04-14/

Washington's role as a global financial regulator." He also stated, "that mass immigration, economic decline, and moral degradation will trigger a civil war next fall and the collapse of the dollar."[332] While Panarin was wrong on the timing (*The Wall Street Journal* article was published in 2008 and forecast American disintegration for 2010), he certainly seems to have been right regarding the direction.

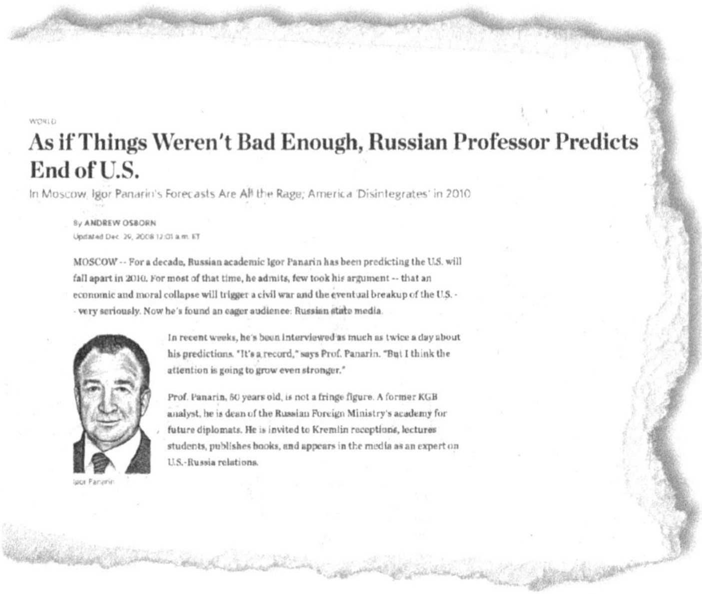

WORLD

As if Things Weren't Bad Enough, Russian Professor Predicts End of U.S.

In Moscow, Igor Panarin's Forecasts Are All the Rage; America 'Disintegrates' in 2010

By ANDREW OSBORN
Updated Dec. 29, 2008 12:01 a.m. ET

MOSCOW -- For a decade, Russian academic Igor Panarin has been predicting the U.S. will fall apart in 2010. For most of that time, he admits, few took his argument -- that an economic and moral collapse will trigger a civil war and the eventual breakup of the U.S. -- very seriously. Now he's found an eager audience: Russian state media.

In recent weeks, he's been interviewed as much as twice a day about his predictions. "It's a record," says Prof. Panarin. "But I think the attention is going to grow even stronger."

Prof. Panarin, 50 years old, is not a fringe figure. A former KGB analyst, he is dean of the Russian Foreign Ministry's academy for future diplomats. He is invited to Kremlin receptions, lectures students, publishes books, and appears in the media as an expert on U.S.-Russia relations.

Igor Panarin

Could that actually happen here? I suppose anything is possible and the case Panarin makes is somewhat compelling. He certainly is on target with the debt part, the failed currency part, the moral decline part, and the mass immigration part. But we still believe the most likely outcome would be a rush to implement Central Bank Digital Currencies (CBDC) with all the control that implies (as we discussed in Chapter Three). That would allow unlimited money creation combined with the social control mechanisms to keep people in line. Throw in Artificial Intelligence and mass surveillance and you get science fiction scary.

332. https://web.archive.org/web/20150731074551/http://www.wsj.com/articles/SB123051100709638419

I told you at the end of Chapter Three that things would seem to get worse and worse as you kept reading. But I also promised that after that, they would get much, much better. So, keep reading, things will turn up! We have an answer, a way of escape, provided by the Founders. Hint: It's a modern form of pirate money! States can make it happen if they learn the truth and find the will to act. They can save America with your help. We will show you how.

NOTE:

If you are a big fan of history and monetary theory, keep reading! You will love Chapters Six and Seven. If that's not your deal and you can take my word that the plan we are outlining is Constitutional and totally legal, then feel free to skip ahead to Chapter Eight, "Economic Justice."

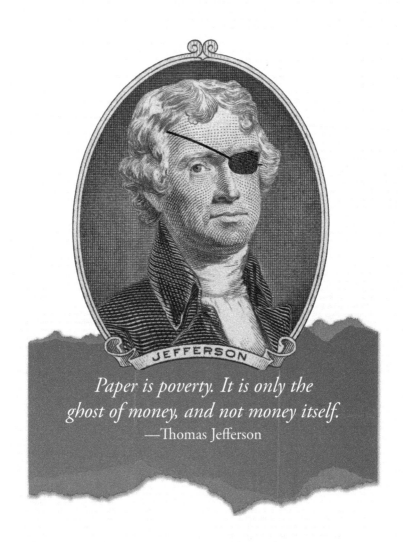

Paper is poverty. It is only the ghost of money, and not money itself.

—Thomas Jefferson

6

THE FOUNDER'S SECRET THAT CAN SAVE AMERICA

The Founders warned us and here we are.

Paper money has had the effect in your state that it will ever have, to ruin commerce, oppress the honest, and open the door to every species of fraud and injustice.

—George Washington in a 1786 letter to Thomas Jefferson[333]

Paper money is unjust. It is unconstitutional, for it affects the rights of property as much as taking away equal value in land.

—James Madison, Chief Architect of the Constitution[334]

333. https://www.nationalreview.com/2011/07/founders-no-fans-paper-currency-deroy-murdock/
334. Ibid

To emit an unfunded paper as the sign of value ought not to continue a formal part of the Constitution, nor ever hereafter to be employed; being, in its nature, pregnant with abuses, and liable to be made the engine of imposition and fraud; holding out temptations equally pernicious to the integrity of government and to the morals of the people.

—Alexander Hamilton, America's first Treasury secretary (immortalized in the Broadway hit *Hamilton*)[335]

To say that the Founders hated unbacked paper money is an understatement. They loathed it. And more importantly, they feared it. They knew the destruction it could bring from addiction to the printing press and the inevitable greed of humanity. But they also understood the necessity and risks of playing with fire for an unprecedented fledgling Republic that was created by "We the People." They had experience with unrestrained paper money and felt the devastating consequences. But they were also "rolling the dice" as to whether United States could form and defend a lasting nation.

NOTE:

You may be thinking of the Founders as a bunch of stuffy, slave-owning patriarchal aristocrats. Or you may consider them the greatest men in history. Neither would be entirely accurate. A fair reading recognizes that the Founders were very human, many young brave rebels.[336,337] Many understood how evil slavery was but were trapped in a system and world very foreign to our 21st century cultural awareness.[338]

335. Ibid

336. https://www.smithsonianmag.com/smart-news/americas-founders-were-scarily-young-on-july-4-1776-28327892/

337. https://allthingsliberty.com/2013/08/ages-of-revolution-how-old-1776/

338. https://historyengine.richmond.edu/episodes/view/4890

NOTE:

Slavery is evil regardless of the time period, and many colonials worked against it.[339] But they all had a passion for liberty and justice and were willing to fight.[340] This is no excuse for allowing evil but 250 years from now we will be judged by that generation's standards and may not fare well.[341] One thing I believe. If they were alive today, the Founders would be intrigued by bitcoin and big fans of decentralized finance.[342] And they would push back hard against CBDC and The Great Reset.[343]

People used to understand the dangers of fiat paper money. Unfortunately, most Americans today don't think twice about it. If they have paper bills at all, that to them is real money. It's what they get when they cash a check or use an ATM. Kind of old fashioned but useful for tips, birthday gifts, and small purchases when you forget your credit card or phone. And people don't even stop to look at the dirty green paper stuffed in their wallets along with a driver's license, health ID, credit cards, and receipts.

339. https://thehill.com/changing-america/opinion/506782-anti-slavery-revolutionaries-who-practiced-what-they-preached/
340. https://www.americanheritage.com/delegates-behind-declaration
341. https://www.prageru.com/video/no-past-no-future
342. https://paxful.com/university/3-things-the-founding-fathers-could-learn-from-bitcoin/
343. https://www.johnlocke.org/the-great-reset-an-attack-on-freedom-and-sovereignty/

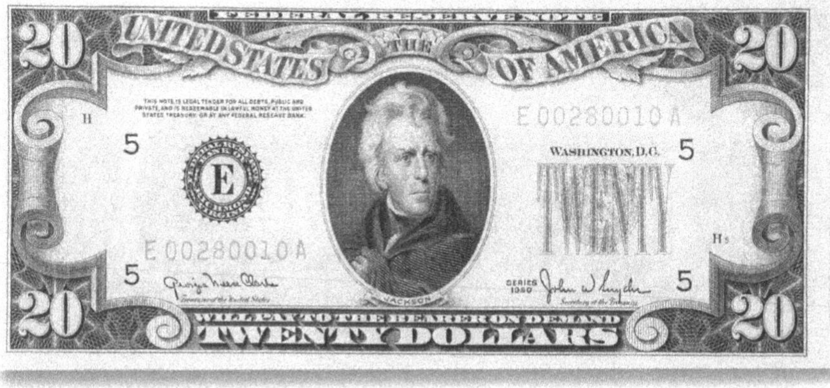

If you have one, pull a "twenty" from your pocket or purse and look at it closely. It says at the top "FEDERAL RESERVE NOTE." Then, on the lower left, printed in small all-cap letters you see, "THIS NOTE IS LEGAL TENDER FOR ALL DEBTS PUBLIC AND PRIVATE." You also see the foreboding seal of the Federal Reserve above that (looks intimidating) and on the right, a green seal of the Department of the Treasury. There are two signatures, one from the Treasurer of the United States and the other from the Secretary of the Treasury. Then, there's the picture of a dead President, in this case, Andrew Jackson.

NOTE:

Jackson, by the way, is certainly among the least favorite presidents to my Cherokee family for his racist "Trail of Tears."[344] But perhaps he was right in his hatred of bankers, Central Banks, and paper money.[345] It's pretty ironic that he's pictured on the most recognized Federal Reserve note in circulation.

344. https://www.pbs.org/wgbh/aia/part4/4h1567.html
345. https://www.seattletimes.com/nation-world/andrew-jackson-populist-war-hero-and-no-fan-of-paper-money

The operative word on the 20-dollar bill is "NOTE." In finance, NOTE refers to a debt instrument. The paper is an IOU or promise to pay back a loan plus any interest due.[346] When issued by a government, however, those IOUs function as money as explained by *Investopedia*:

> *A banknote is a negotiable promissory note which one party can use to pay another party a specific amount of money. A banknote is payable to the bearer on demand, and the amount payable is apparent on the face of the note. Banknotes are considered legal tender; along with coins, they make up the bearer forms of all modern money. A banknote is known as a "bill" or a "note."...*
>
> *In the U.S., only the Federal Reserve Bank is allowed to print banknotes for money.*
>
> *While banknotes used to be backed by precious metals such as gold and silver, in 1971, the United States government went off the gold standard, making American banknotes a fiat currency that is backed instead by good faith.*[347]

Federal Reserve Notes are debt instruments. They used to be a promise to pay the bearer in gold and silver. But now, they can't be redeemed. The best you can get is two tens for your twenty or a combination of tens, fives, and ones that add up to twenty. But if you want "real money" (aka gold and silver), forget about it.

Just to be sure, I am NOT saying that Federal Reserve Notes aren't legal tender in today's America. They are, even though a

346. https://corporatefinanceinstitute.com/resources/capital-markets/note/
347. https://www.investopedia.com/terms/b/banknote.asp

small group of vocal detractors would disagree.[348] They are money because the Congress has the power to coin money and that has been interpreted by the courts as including the power to print bills and notes as well.[349]

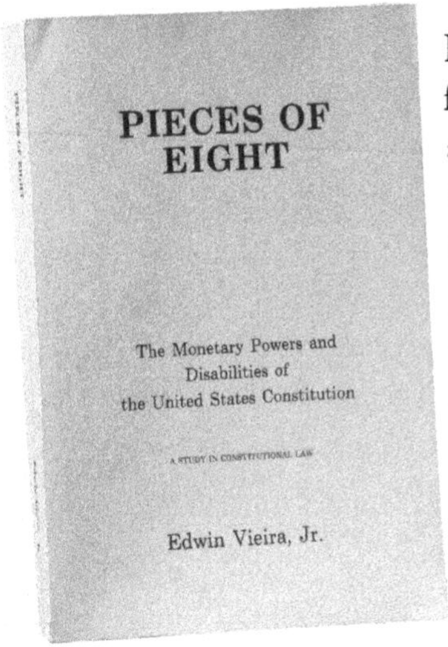

Having said that upfront, it is important for you to understand how we got here and that can guide us on how we get out of the mess we are in. You could buy a copy of the definitive work on the monetary powers and disabilities of the United States Constitution by Edwin Vieira, Jr. titled *Pieces of Eight* (note the "pirate money" reference). It's rare and out of print but you can pick up a copy on Amazon for $400 or $500 (presumably less if you pay in silver coin).[350] I opted for the paperback. Vieira has four degrees from Harvard and had his work submitted to President Reagan's United States Gold Commission that reported to Congress in 1982.[351] Commission member, Congressman Ron Paul, wrote the Foreword when it debuted as *Pieces of Eight* the following year. Vieira also later wrote *The Forgotten Role of the Constitution in Monetary Law* published in the Texas Review of Law and Politics.[352]

I've spent hundreds of hours poring through Vieira's work and also reviewing multiple Supreme Court cases as well as the writings of the Founders, monetary experts, and historians. They don't always agree or interpret things the same way. But I like Vieira a great deal and adding a touch of real-world truth from history paints a clear picture of our current monetary mess and how we got here.

348. https://i2i.org/new-evidence-on-the-constitutionality-of-paper-money/
349. https://constitution.findlaw.com/article1/annotation37.html
350. https://www.amazon.com/Pieces-Eight-Disabilities-Constitution-Foundation/dp/0967175917
351. https://images.procon.org/wp-content/uploads/sites/23/gold_comission_report_1982.pdf
352. https://www.famguardian.org/Subjects/MoneyBanking/Money/VieraTexasLawReview.pdf

Let's review some historical facts.

1. The Continental Congress did, in an act of desperation, print quite a lot of paper money with a promise to repay in gold or silver. It was an economic disaster. I picked up a 1776 Four-dollar Continental Note on eBay originally printed in Philadelphia. It was a promise to pay the bearer four Spanish milled dollars (pieces of eight pirate money) or the value in gold or silver. Says so right on the front! Unfortunately, the Continental Congress was not good for it. They had only one or two pennies of silver behind every paper dollar. That's where the old-timey saying, "Not worth a Continental," comes from.[353] It's also why you can buy original Continentals on eBay today. George Washington once noted that it would take more than a wagonload of Continentals to buy one wagonload of supplies.[354]

353. https://www.aier.org/article/not-worth-a-continental
354. Ibid

2. During the Articles of Confederation, paper money nearly bankrupted our new nation. Not only did the Congress coin and print money, but so did the states with varying levels of control. This created mass economic chaos and was one of the primary reasons for the failure of the Articles.[355] Commerce was threatened by having 14 different types (13 states plus the Feds) of government money available plus foreign and private money, each with different levels of soundness and backing. This led to the Economic Crisis of the 1780s.[356] Eventually, the states and nation had enough, creating a call for a Constitutional Convention.[357] This also led to the 1785 adoption by Congress of the Spanish milled dollar (aka piece of eight, aka "peso") as the official currency and unit of value for American money. It was designated by weight and purity (0.7734 troy ounces) of fine silver. Gold coins were allowed as well but they were valued in relation to the silver dollar. In fact, all American money, including the name dollar, was based on this.[358] And it served our nation for over seven decades until the Coinage Act of 1857 which outlawed the use of foreign coins.[359]

3. **At the Constitutional Convention, there were hot debates over whether or not to issue unbacked paper money.** At one point in the drafting process, language was added specifically allowing Congress the power to "emit bills of credit." That language was struck nearly unanimously after an impassioned speech by Gouverneur Morris (delegate from Pennsylvania), leaving neither endorsement nor prohibition for the Congress.[360] Maybe it was thought sufficient that because the power was not granted, it was denied. But to others who came later, the door was left open if ever needed. Either way, the

355. https://classroom.synonym.com/did-articles-confederation-give-congress-power-issue-currency-12668.html
356. https://alphahistory.com/americanrevolution/economic-crisis-of-the-1780s/
357. https://history.state.gov/milestones/1784-1800/convention-and-ratification
358. https://www.cmi-gold-silver.com/history-american-money/
359. https://www.rarecollectiblestv.com/blog/the-lasting-impact-of-the-coinage-act-of-1857.html
360. https://fee.org/articles/fiat-and-the-founding-fathers/

final version of the Constitution expressly forbade states from emitting bills of credit (paper money) but was silent regarding Congressional authority to do so. Spanish coins remained the standard and the word dollar was enshrined as our national monetary unit. The United States government did not issue purely paper money for nearly three-quarters of a century.[361] Instead, private banks issued paper redeemable in gold or silver that circulated as currency. This created confusion and concerns over private bank risk and soundness.[362] But silver pieces of eight (aka dollars) remained the standard.

4. In order to pay the high costs of the Civil War, both North and South issued paper money whose value rose and fell as the fortunes of war shifted.[363] Private banks no longer converted paper money to coins or gold and silver on demand leading to a crisis.[364] The National Currency (Banking) Act was passed in 1863, replacing private notes with Federal paper.[365,366]

5. The Supreme Court ruled in 1870 that unbacked paper money was unconstitutional (Hepburn v. Griswold). Their decision was based on the idea that fiat money (greenbacks) represented an unlawful taking in violation of the Fifth Amendment Due Process Clause. That ruling was quickly overturned in the next Court session (1871 in the Knox-Parker decision) after Republican President Ulysses S. Grant packed the Supreme Court with two new justices, paving the road to fiat money.[367,368]

---

361. https://www.cmi-gold-silver.com/history-american-money/
362. https://www.marketwatch.com/story/the-history-of-private-bank-notes-in-1800s-may-hint-at-the-future-for-stablecoins-not-a-good-one-says-goldman-sachs-11652830513
363. https://www.investopedia.com/ask/answers/09/paper-money-usa.asp
364. https://www.encyclopedia.com/history/encyclopedias-almanacs-transcripts-and-maps/national-bank-act-1863
365. https://www.marketwatch.com/story/the-history-of-private-bank-notes-in-1800s-may-hint-at-the-future-for-stablecoins-not-a-good-one-says-goldman-sachs-11652830513
366. https://www.occ.treas.gov/about/who-we-are/history/founding-occ-national-bank-system/index-founding-occ-national-banking-system.html
367. https://constitutingamerica.org/the-legal-tender-cases-1870-guest-essayist-kevin-walsh/
368. https://constitutioncenter.org/blog/packing-the-supreme-court-explained

6. The Federal Reserve was established by Congress in 1913 and has become the de-facto monopoly supplier of American money even if privately owned by member banks.[369,370] The Federal Reserve authorizes the production of notes, commonly known as dollar bills, two-dollar bills, five-dollar bills, ten-dollar bills, twenty-dollar bills, fifty-dollar bills, and 100-dollar bills. Initially the Fed was required to hold gold reserves capable of redeeming 40% of outstanding bills although that was later abandoned.[371]

   From *Investopedia:*

   > *Before 1971, each Federal Reserve note issued was backed by a legally specified amount of gold held by the U.S. Treasury, however, (after 1933) private citizens were not allowed to redeem notes for gold dollars. Because these notes held legal tender status and represented actual dollars, they were commonly referred to as "dollar bills" as they circulated through the economy. However, under President Nixon, the gold standard was officially abandoned, creating a full fiat currency, where the Federal Reserve notes themselves are the sole circulating legal tender, along with small base-metal coins.*[372]

7. Separate from the Federal Reserve, the United States Treasury also issued bills and paper certificates starting in 1862. These were convertible to real money (gold and silver) and were (and remain) legal tender. They are now rare and out of circulation and no longer convertible to precious metal.[373] But you can still pick up copies at coin shops and antique malls. You can spend them. But why

369. https://www.federalreserve.gov/aboutthefed/fract.htm
370. https://www.frbsf.org/education/publications/doctor-econ/2003/september/private-public-corporation/
371. https://www.marketplace.org/2023/07/07/why-are-federal-reserve-regional-banks-listed-on-us-currency/
372. https://www.investopedia.com/terms/f/federal-reserve-note.asp
373. https://www.thermofisher.com/blog/metals/is-us-currency-still-backed-by-gold-and-if-so-where-is-it-all/

would you? The collectible value is far above face value.

From *Investopedia*:

> *A U.S. Note was an earlier form of paper money in the U.S. from 1862-1971, which was backed by and redeemable for physical silver or gold. Between 1933 and 1971 both United States Notes and Federal Reserve Notes were considered legal tender.*

8. On April 5, 1933, President Franklin Roosevelt signed Executive Order 6102 "forbidding the hoarding of gold coin, gold bullion, and gold certificates within the continental United States." This not only ended gold convertibility of Federal Reserve and U.S. Treasury notes but also led to the confiscation of gold from citizens.[374]

> *All persons are hereby required to deliver on or before May 1, 1933, to a Federal Reserve Bank or a branch or agency thereof or to any member bank of the Federal Reserve System all gold coin, gold bullion and gold certificates now owned by them or coming into their ownership on or before April 28, 1933...*[375]

374. https://www.sbcgold.com/blog/a-dangerous-precedent-executive-order-6102/
375. https://www.sbcgold.com/gold-confiscation/executive-order-6102/

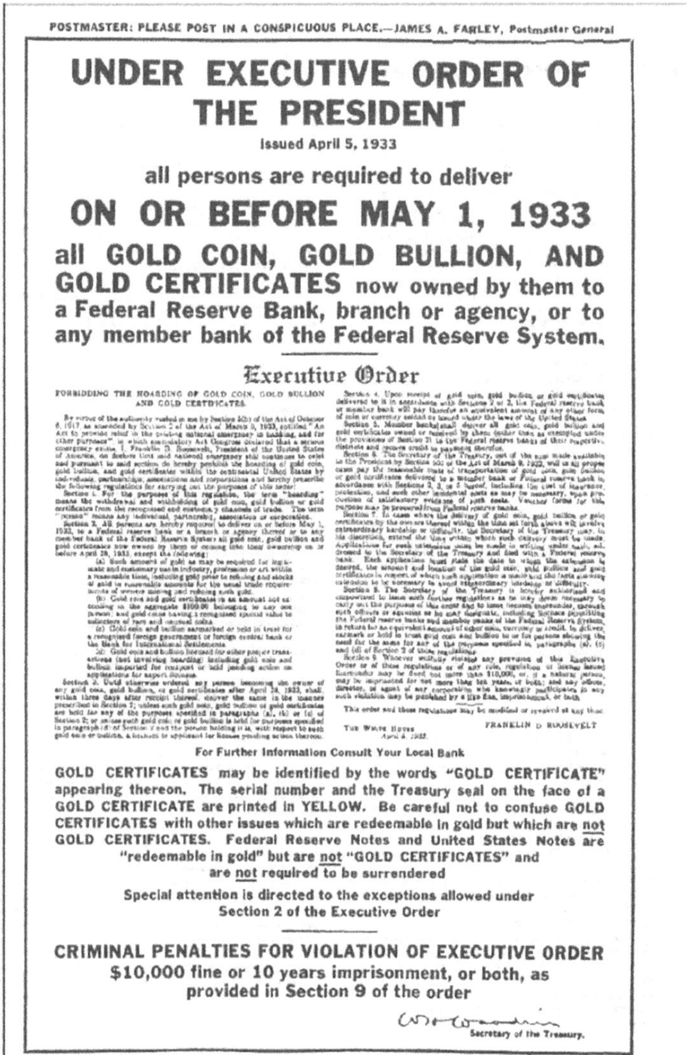

POSTMASTER: PLEASE POST IN A CONSPICUOUS PLACE.—JAMES A. FARLEY, Postmaster General

UNDER EXECUTIVE ORDER OF THE PRESIDENT

Issued April 5, 1933

all persons are required to deliver

ON OR BEFORE MAY 1, 1933

all GOLD COIN, GOLD BULLION, AND GOLD CERTIFICATES now owned by them to a Federal Reserve Bank, branch or agency, or to any member bank of the Federal Reserve System.

Executive Order

FORBIDDING THE HOARDING OF GOLD COIN, GOLD BULLION AND GOLD CERTIFICATES.

By virtue of the authority vested in me by Section 5(b) of the Act of October 6, 1917, as amended by Section 2 of the Act of March 9, 1933, entitled "An Act to provide relief in the existing national emergency in banking, and for other purposes", in which amendatory Act Congress declared that a serious emergency exists, I, Franklin D. Roosevelt, President of the United States of America, do declare that said national emergency still continues to exist and pursuant to said section do hereby prohibit the hoarding of gold coin, gold bullion, and gold certificates within the continental United States by individuals, partnerships, associations and corporations and hereby prescribe the following regulations for carrying out the purposes of this order:

Section 1. For the purposes of this regulation, the term "hoarding" means the withdrawal and withholding of gold coin, gold bullion or gold certificates from the recognized and customary channels of trade. The term "person" means any individual, partnership, association or corporation.

Section 2. All persons are hereby required to deliver on or before May 1, 1933, to a Federal reserve bank or a branch or agency thereof or to any member bank of the Federal Reserve System all gold coin, gold bullion and gold certificates now owned by them or coming into their ownership on or before April 28, 1933, except the following:

(a) Such amount of gold as may be required for legitimate and customary use in industry, profession or art within a reasonable time, including gold prior to refining and stocks of gold in reasonable amounts for the usual trade requirements of owners mining and refining such gold.

(b) Gold coin and gold certificates in an amount not exceeding in the aggregate $100.00 belonging to any one person; and gold coins having a recognized special value to collectors of rare and unusual coins.

(c) Gold coin and bullion earmarked or held in trust for a recognized foreign government or foreign central bank or the Bank for International Settlements.

(d) Gold coin and bullion licensed for other proper transactions (not involving hoarding) including gold coin and bullion imported for reexport or held pending action on applications for export licenses.

Section 3. Until otherwise ordered any person becoming the owner of any gold coin, gold bullion, or gold certificates after April 28, 1933, shall, within three days after receipt thereof, deliver the same in the manner prescribed in Section 2; unless such gold coin, gold bullion or gold certificates are held for any of the purposes specified in paragraphs (a), (b) or (c) of Section 2; or unless such gold coin or gold bullion is held for purposes specified in paragraph (d) of Section 2 and the person holding it is, with respect to such gold coin or bullion, a licensee or applicant for license pending action thereon.

Section 4. Upon receipt of gold coin, gold bullion, or gold certificates delivered to it in accordance with Sections 2 or 3, the Federal reserve bank or member bank will pay therefor an equivalent amount of any other form of coin or currency coined or issued under the laws of the United States.

Section 5. Member banks shall deliver all gold coin, gold bullion and gold certificates owned or received by them (other than as exempted under the provisions of Section 2) to the Federal reserve banks of their respective districts and receive credit or payment therefor.

Section 6. The Secretary of the Treasury, out of the sum made available to the President by Section 501 of the Act of March 9, 1933, will in all proper cases pay the reasonable costs of transportation of gold coin, gold bullion or gold certificates delivered to a member bank or Federal reserve bank in accordance with Sections 2, 3, or 5 hereof, including the cost of insurance, protection, and such other incidental costs as may be necessary, upon production of satisfactory evidence of such costs. Voucher forms for this purpose may be procured from Federal reserve banks.

Section 7. In cases where the delivery of gold coin, gold bullion or gold certificates by the owners thereof within the time set forth above will involve extraordinary hardship or difficulty, the Secretary of the Treasury may, in his discretion, extend the time within which such delivery must be made. Applications for such extensions must be made in writing under oath, addressed to the Secretary of the Treasury and filed with a Federal reserve bank. Each application must state the date to which the extension is desired, the amount and location of the gold coin, gold bullion and gold certificates in respect of which such application is made and the facts showing extension to be necessary to avoid extraordinary hardship or difficulty.

Section 8. The Secretary of the Treasury is hereby authorized and empowered to issue such further regulations as he may deem necessary to carry out the purposes of this order and to issue licenses thereunder, through such officers or agencies as he may designate, including licenses permitting the Federal reserve banks and member banks of the Federal Reserve System, in return for an equivalent amount of other coin, currency or credit, to deliver, earmark or hold in trust gold coin and bullion to or for persons showing the need for the same for any of the purposes specified in paragraphs (a), (c) and (d) of Section 2 of these regulations.

Section 9. Whoever willfully violates any provision of this Executive Order or of these regulations or of any rule, regulation or license issued thereunder may be fined not more than $10,000, or, if a natural person, may be imprisoned for not more than ten years, or both; and any officer, director, or agent of any corporation who knowingly participates in any such violation may be punished by a like fine, imprisonment, or both.

This order and these regulations may be modified or revoked at any time.

FRANKLIN D ROOSEVELT

THE WHITE HOUSE
April 5, 1933.

For Further Information Consult Your Local Bank

GOLD CERTIFICATES may be identified by the words "GOLD CERTIFICATE" appearing thereon. The serial number and the Treasury seal on the face of a GOLD CERTIFICATE are printed in YELLOW. Be careful not to confuse GOLD CERTIFICATES with other issues which are redeemable in gold but which are not GOLD CERTIFICATES. Federal Reserve Notes and United States Notes are "redeemable in gold" but are not "GOLD CERTIFICATES" and are not required to be surrendered

Special attention is directed to the exceptions allowed under Section 2 of the Executive Order

CRIMINAL PENALTIES FOR VIOLATION OF EXECUTIVE ORDER $10,000 fine or 10 years imprisonment, or both, as provided in Section 9 of the order

W. H. Woodin
Secretary of the Treasury.

U.S. Government Printing Office: 1933 2-16064

The Federal Government did pay (in paper bills and coin) the amount of $20.67 per troy ounce. After this, the Treasury only issued Silver Certificates. In 1934, the government increased the price per ounce of gold to $35 with the Gold Reserve Act.[376] People felt cheated as the gold they

376. https://www.federalreservehistory.org/essays/gold-reserve-act

had surrendered just a year earlier was increased in value, essentially making the paper money they were given worthless.

9. President Nixon ended any form of convertibility to gold in 1971 as a "temporary" measure.[377,378] While citizens could not redeem paper money for gold after 1933, the Treasury did allow foreign governments that opportunity.[379] With inflation building, many foreign nations, led by Charles de Gaulle of France, decided they would rather have gold than dollars.[380] The demand to withdraw was so great that Nixon feared it would bankrupt the Treasury, so he closed the gold window. It was supposed to be a temporary measure.

   Shortly afterward, however, Nixon's Secretary of State Henry Kissinger crafted a new way to support our currency. He created the "petrodollar" arrangement where Saudi Arabia was protected by America and agreed to price oil exclusively in dollars and to reinvest any excess financial reserves back into U.S. Treasury bonds.[381] That arrangement stood for 50 years. Now, however, the Saudis have not only agreed to price oil in Chinese yuan but also have agreed to join the BRICS alliance.[382] Some believe this is because America has pivoted in the Middle East more towards Iran.[383] Others suggest that they recognize the excessive Federal Debt and need to hedge their currency bet.[384]

377. https://schiffgold.com/commentaries/an-inauspicious-anniversary-nixon-slams-shut-the-gold-window/
378. https://journals.sagepub.com/doi/pdf/10.1177/2378023119841812
379. https://mises.org/wire/today-1971-president-nixon-closes-gold-window
380. https://content.time.com/time/subscriber/article/0,33009,840572,00.html
381. https://www.sandstoneam.com/insight/rise-of-the-petrodollar
382. https://www.forbes.com/sites/greatspeculations/2023/03/27/petrodollar-dusk-petroyuan-dawn-what-investors-need-to-know
383. https://www.iiss.org/en/online-analysis/survival-online/2022/12/fraught-relations-saudi-ambitions-and-american-anger/
384. https://fanack.com/economy/features-insights/arab-countries-most-vulnerable-to-us-public-debt-risks-252083/

10. Biden Bucks (CBDC) soon will be issued by the Federal Reserve and will function as money, untethered to gold or silver, and not even limited by paper or ink.

Here we are today. Our money has no backing other than confidence (which is faltering). Other nations want to remake the global monetary system. The petrodollar is ending. Fiat paper money is being phased out by electronic versions. And we are on the cusp of Central Bank Digital Currency issued by the Federal Reserve with unlimited creation and total draconian control provided to the Federal Government (as we discussed in Chapter Three).

Does this mean the Founders warned us and then stuck us with an evil fiat monetary system from which we cannot escape? Say it isn't so! And isn't this supposed to be the chapter where things start to look better? Hang on…it's coming!

The Founders Did Provide a Way of Escape

While the Founders prevented states from either "coining money," or "emitting bills of credit," they did allow one single provision for states regarding money. In just a few words, they provided what can be our escape hatch. Maybe our "safe space." And because they were so specific, it should actually work.

The prohibition against coining money was obvious at the time. If a Spanish milled dollar contained 0.7734 troy ounces of fine silver, they did not want the confusion if a New York dollar held 0.45 troy ounces of silver and a Massachusetts dollar had 0.25 ounces. They were concerned that states might "debase" the currency. Debasing refers to the notion of adding base metal in coinage, lowering the precious metal content.

And, while the Constitution is silent regarding Congress' ability to emit bills of credit (that is producing unbacked paper money), it was quite specific in preventing states from doing so. Allowing states to issue bills of credit was a big failure of the Articles of Confederation that the Founders did not want repeated. States would not produce unbacked paper money. Period.

The ONLY thing states were allowed to do about money was delineated in Article 1, Section 10. And what was described was in the form of a negative.

> ***No State shall*** *enter into any Treaty, Alliance, or Confederation; grant Letters of Marque and Reprisal; coin Money; emit Bills of Credit;* ***make any Thing but gold and silver Coin a Tender in Payment of Debts****; pass any Bill of Attainder, ex post facto Law, or Law impairing the Obligation of Contracts, or grant any Title of Nobility.*[385]

While Congress has authority regarding money, the states are boxed in. They can't print bills. They can't coin copper pennies (or nickel nickels). But, by default, they can make gold and silver coins to be legal tender. In other words, they can make real money (pirate money like gold doubloons and silver pieces of eight) legal tender by force of law. And the Federal Government has absolutely no say about it as this is essentially an enumerated power provided to the states.

At first, states simply followed the lead of Congress which made the Spanish milled dollar the currency of the United States.[386]

385. https://constitution.congress.gov/browse/article-1/section-10
386. https://www.iberdrola.com/culture/spanish-dollar

PIRATE FUN FACT: If you are wondering why the term "milled" is used in reference to the Spanish dollar, it is because these dollars were produced by machine rather than by hand indicating uniformity.[387] They had a set silver content and a ridged pattern around the circumference. This discouraged "clipping" where thieves would shave a piece of precious metal from each coin. Milled coins were perfectly round and of uniform size so any clipping could be seen visually.

Over time, Congress would authorize the minting of purely American coins and, when a sufficient number were in circulation, they outlawed foreign coins.[388] The Coinage Act of 1857 ended the use of foreign coin as legal tender in America.[389] And then, decades ago, the U.S. Government stopped producing gold and silver coins for monetary use.[390] This leaves Federal Reserve notes and debased coins (without gold or silver) as the only money available. And don't forget that states are prohibited from coining their own money under Article 1, Section 10.

All of this sort of boxes the states out of the money equation ... Or does it???

There must be an answer. We'll find out in Chapter Seven!

387. https://coinparade.co.uk/what-is-milled-coinage/
388. https://www.usmint.gov/learn/history/historical-documents/legislation-to-allow-foreign-coins-as-legal-tender
389. https://www.rarecollectiblestv.com/blog/the-lasting-impact-of-the-coinage-act-of-1857.html
390. https://www.moneymetals.com/news/2016/03/23/history-junk-silver-90-percent-coins-000845

GOLD CERTIFICATE FROM 1934

GOLD CERTIFICATE FROM 1928

Images: *National Numismatic Collection, National Museum of American History, Smithsonian Institution.*

Gold is money.
Everything else is credit.
—J.P. Morgan, Congressional Testimony (1912)

7

The Power Reserved to States

What's a State to Do?

If states are boxed in to only make gold and silver coins as legal tender and boxed out of using coins (because none are available and states can't make them), it seems like "Game Over." But the Founders felt differently, and the courts have through the years made that clear. There is an escape from monetary hell. And it is gold and silver. Let me explain.

1. The Constitutional prohibition against a state coining money was primarily with the intent of preventing debasement as noted in Joseph Story's 1833 Commentaries on the Constitution of the United States:

In order to secure it from debasement it is necessary, that it should be exclusively under the control and regulation of the (federal) government; for if every individual were permitted to make and circulate, what coin he should please, there would be an opening to the grossest frauds and impositions upon the public, by the use of base and false coin ... The varying standards and regulations of the different states would introduce infinite embarrassments and vexations in the course of trade; and often subject the innocent to the grossest frauds.[391]

2. States were not, however, prohibited from making foreign gold and silver coin to be legal tender. The point was really uniformity, not who minted the coin. The Founders clearly did not prefer Spain over Virginia or New Jersey. Rather, they wanted simplicity and uniformity so that the citizens of one state might have confidence in the coins used in another. Multiple kinds of money were circulating at the time, federal, foreign, and private.[392] But the only money a state could make legal tender would be gold and silver coins. Initially, these were gold doubloons and silver pieces of eight (aka pirate money).[393,394]

3. Because it was difficult and risky to carry gold and silver coins, many states created banks which stored coins and produced essentially "warehouse receipts" for gold and silver deposited there. The receipts functioned as money. They could be traded as legal tender currency and tendered for gold and silver coin at the bank on demand. These receipts were not considered "bills of credit" as long as there were coins held at the state bank on a one-for-one basis. They were more akin to the silver certificates our Treasury used to produce.

391. https://press-pubs.uchicago.edu/founders/documents/a1_8_5s10.html
392. https://www.clevelandfed.org/en/publications/economic-commentary/2007/ec-20070101-private-money-in-our-past-present-and-future
393. https://www.greatamericancoincompany.com/a/info/blog/what-is-a-dubloon
394. https://www.we-heart.com/2022/11/28/what-are-gold-doubloons-real-most-expensive/

On eBay, I bought a 1837 Bank of Kentucky 12.5 cent note. It was redeemable for one pie slice from a piece of eight (1/8th of a Spanish dollar) when presented for payment at the bank.

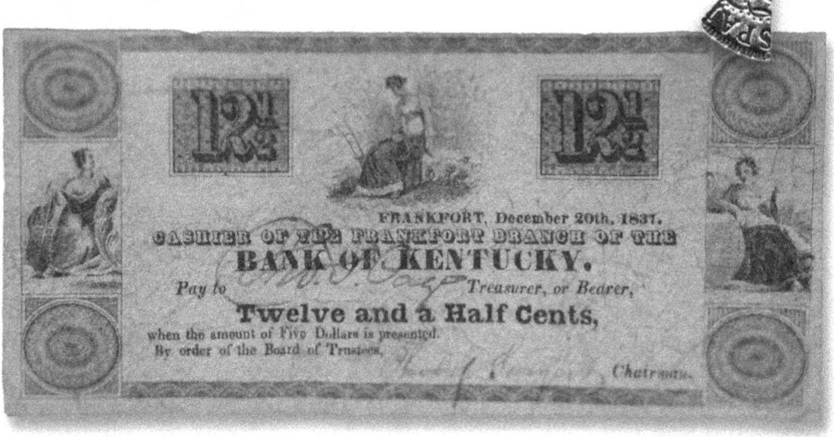

The Bank of Kentucky became perhaps the most famous of the state-chartered banks due to an 1837 case, *Briscoe v. Bank of Kentucky*, that reached the Supreme Court. It seems that John Briscoe did not believe the Bank of Kentucky's notes were Constitutional. He read that states could not emit bills of credit. He had a scheme to borrow from the Bank, spend the notes, and refuse to repay what he believed was unconstitutional and thus worthless paper.[395,396]

Despite the Constitutional prohibition against bills of credit, the Court ruled 6-1 that the Bank of Kentucky notes were legal tender, and the debt must be repaid. The lone dissent was Justice Story (quoted above in point one) who believed that Kentucky was producing impermissible state currency.[397]

395. Finkelman, Paul; Urofsky, Melvin I. (2003). Landmark Decisions of the United States Supreme Court, https://archive.org/details/landmarkdecision0000fink. Washington, DC: CQ Press. pp. 46–47. ISBN 978-1-56802-720-3.

396. https://en.m.wikipedia.org/wiki/Briscoe_v._Bank_of_Kentucky

397. McDonald, Forrest (2000). States' Rights and the Union: Imperium in Imperio, https://archive.org/details/statesrightsun00mcdo, 1776–1876. Lawrence, KS: University Press of Kansas. p. 128. ISBN 978-0-7006-1040-2.

The majority, however, felt that the bank (although owned entirely by the state) was a separate entity and able to be sued apart from the state. This meant that its notes were not bills of credit emitted by the state.[398] Further, because the notes were redeemable in gold and silver coin, they conformed to the Constitutional guidelines.[399] As shared by Richard Timberlake in *The Significance of Unaccounted Currencies*:

> *The notes [of the bank, in the case of Briscoe vs. Bank of Kentucky] were not only payable in gold and silver on demand," argued Justice McLean, "but there was a ... sufficient fund to redeem them.*[400]

The Briscoe decision was monumental in enabling states to produce money, an essential part of the emerging United States economy. This decision came from a Jacksonian Court that shared Jackson's distrust of a Central Bank and preferred states' rights. This decision has never been challenged and has been cited multiple times in modern rulings. Based on the Bank of Kentucky decision, it is clear that a state could take gold and silver coins on deposit and issue the equivalent of warehouse receipts that the state could then declare as legal tender.

4. But what if there were no coins to deposit? That became a dilemma once foreign coins were no longer allowed as tender and when the Federal government stopped producing useful gold and silver coins. Fortunately, the Supreme Court rendered another favorable decision that answered this challenge. In Bronson v. Rodes (1868), the Court was faced with a dilemma. A contract had been struck, payable in specific gold and silver coinage. When the debt was

398. Baxter, Maurice G. (2000). Henry Clay the Lawyer, https://archive.org/details/henryclaylawyer00baxt. Lexington, KY: University Press of Kentucky. pp. 70–75. ISBN 978-0-8131-2147-5.
399. https://casetext.com/case/briscoe-v-the-bank-of-the-commonwealth-of-kentucky
400. https://www.jstor.org/stable/2120649

repaid, however, it was done so with United States notes deemed legal tender. Was that lawful? The Court ruled it was, so long as the notes were redeemable in bullion equal in weight and quality to the coins listed in the contract.

From the majority opinion written by the Chief Justice:

> *The design of all this minuteness and strictness in the regulation of coinage is easily seen. It indicates the intention of the legislature to give a sure guaranty to the people that the coins made current in payments contain the precise weight of gold or silver of the precise degree of purity declared by the statute.* ***It recognizes the fact, accepted by all men throughout the world, that value is inherent in the precious metals; that gold and silver are in themselves values, and being such, and being in other respects best adapted to the purpose, are the only proper measures of value; that these values are determined by weight and purity; and that form and impress are simply certificates of value, worthy of absolute reliance only because of the known integrity and good faith of the government which gives them.***
>
> ***The propositions just stated are believed to be incontestable.*** *If they are so in fact, the inquiry concerning the legal import of the phrase "dollars payable in gold and silver coin, lawful money of the United States," may be answered without much difficulty. Every such dollar is a piece of gold or silver, certified to be of a certain weight and purity, by the form and impress given to it at the mint of the United States, and therefore declared to be legal tender in payments. Any number of such dollars is the number of grains of standard gold or silver in one dollar multiplied by the given number.*
>
> *Payment of money is delivery by the debtor to the creditor of the amount due.* ***A contract to pay a certain number of dollars in***

> ***gold or silver coins is therefore in legal import, nothing else than an agreement to deliver a certain weight of standard gold, to be ascertained by a count of coins, each of which is certified to contain a definite proportion of that weight. It is not distinguishable, as we think, in principle, from a contract to deliver an equal weight of bullion of equal fineness.*** *It is distinguishable, in circumstance, only by the fact that the sufficiency of the amount to be tendered in payment must be ascertained, in the case of bullion, by assay and the scales, while in the case of coin it may be ascertained by count.*[401]

This decision is also monumental. It frees states from the technicalities of Coin to meet the Constitutional requirement when declaring tender. Purity of bullion and weight are deemed by the Court as equivalent to Coin. Thus, "pirate money" can be doubloons or pieces of eight. Or it can be measured in ounces of gold and silver. Like Briscoe, this ruling remains valid.

5. When you put this all together, you get the basis for modern "pirate money" declared by a state as legal tender in the form of gold and silver bullion. The state can issue warehouse receipts for that bullion that are also legal tender under the Constitution. And those receipts don't have to be paper! They can be electronic. This becomes the ideal form of money we described in Chapter One. This is what money should be!

Let's consider the benefits. First, this money protects against inflation as we've already seen. The silver in ten pre-1964 dimes (face value of $1) can still buy 5 gallons of gasoline today, worth maybe $20. This money is a wonderful store of value.

Second, this money can be made legal tender by a state without interference from the Federal Government. That makes it an ideal

401. https://supreme.justia.com/cases/federal/us/74/229/

alternative to both fiat money and the coming CBDC.

Third, this money is convenient. You can deposit gold and silver (or cash and ask the depository to buy gold and silver on your behalf) and later spend it for groceries, gas, rent, or even a stick of gum using a debit card. The bullion can be exchanged into any currency at the current rate. Thus, it is a valid means of exchange. We've shown that the technology exists and works.

Fourth, it can be denominated by weight (either grams or ounces) that is infinitely divisible (like bitcoin). You can do business with 1/10,000th of an ounce if you'd like, making it a reliable unit of account. Now combine that with a state-based depository and you have a powerful monetary system meeting the standards of the Federal Reserve:

> *To summarize, money has taken many forms through the ages, but money consistently has three functions: store of value, unit of account, and medium of exchange.*[402]

Best of all, as valid legal tender in the United States, this form of gold and silver should not be taxable as a commodity or collectible. Even if declared a "digital asset" (like bitcoin), the IRS specifically excludes legal tender from being taxable! From the IRS Virtual Currency Guidance:

> *The Internal Revenue Service (IRS) is aware that "virtual currency" may be used to pay for goods or services, or held for investment. Virtual currency is a digital representation of value that functions as a medium of exchange, a unit of account, and/or a store of value. In some environments, it operates like "real" currency — i.e., the coin and paper money of the United States or of any other country that is designated as legal tender,*

402. https://www.stlouisfed.org/en/education/economic-lowdown-podcast-series/episode-9-functions-of-money

> *circulates, and is customarily used and accepted as a medium of exchange in the country of issuance—**but it does not have legal tender status in any jurisdiction.** Virtual currency that has an equivalent value in real currency, or that acts as a substitute for real currency, is referred to as "convertible" virtual currency. Bitcoin is one example of a convertible virtual currency. Bitcoin can be digitally traded between users and can be purchased for, or exchanged into, U.S. dollars, Euros, and other real or virtual currencies … In general, the sale or exchange of convertible virtual currency, or the use of convertible virtual currency to pay for goods or services in a real-world economy transaction, has tax consequences that may result in a tax liability.*[403]

The distinction here is an important one. A private entity can offer cryptocurrency or digital assets that function as virtual currency but cannot be legal tender. But, based on the Constitution (Article 1, Section 10) plus the rulings of *Briscoe* and *Bronson*, a state may make physical gold and silver coins or bullion legal tender as well as the receipts that represent them. While there will no doubt be discussion in the courts, it may well be that this legal tender will be exempt from capital gain taxation even if Federal fiat money depreciates against it.

From a moral view, why should you be taxed simply because your money retains its value? And this would be valid legal tender under the Constitution. That has never been taxed in history and a strong case can be made legally that it never should be taxed.

It now becomes obvious that state-based monetized gold and silver are vastly superior to traditional holdings of coin or bullion. The tax advantages alone would make people prefer to hold their gold in a state-based depository. But so will the ability to spend it. I had a client who passed away, leaving three rolls of gold coins in her safe. It took her estate weeks to find a fair price, get a buyer, and then get paid.

403. https://www.irs.gov/irb/2014-16_IRB#NOT-2014-21

NOTE:

Many states have passed laws to make gold and silver coins legal tender. Unfortunately, because they don't "function" as money in a practical sense, the IRS views them as a collectible rather than money, allowing them to be taxed as such.[404] *Our plan makes gold and silver functional in a very real sense and once widely adopted could qualify to meet the Court standards.*[405]

Is This Just Some Crazy Idea?

While I've been studying this idea since I was a kid and really focusing on it since 2008, I was heartened when doing the research for this book. I was diving headlong into the works of Edwin Vieira, Jr. (mentioned earlier) and came across something he wrote that was published in the *Cato Journal* in the Spring/Summer of 2015. Amazingly, he put forth virtually the same idea I just shared with you. More than that, he promoted it as the best solution to an out-of-control, bloated federal bureaucracy.

Vieira is a Constitutional and monetary expert. He holds four degrees from Harvard and has been widely cited at the highest levels. He sees the problem clearly; how unrestrained fiat money threatens the currency and economy but benefits a "vast centralized and consolidated government" no longer beholden in service to the people. He offers two valid solutions:

> *(1) Reforming the Federal Reserve system by introducing a redeemable currency somehow "backed" by gold, and preferably*

404. https://www.irs.gov/individuals/international-taxpayers/foreign-currency-and-currency-exchange-rates
405. https://www.law.cornell.edu/uscode/text/26/985

> *by silver as well, because no monometallic gold standard can exist under the Constitution; and (2) replacing the present monetary regime with an entirely new system of economically sound, honest, and especially constitutional money.*[406]

He focuses his article on the second option, deeming it more likely. To accomplish that, he suggests three possibilities and then dismisses the potential for the first two. The first option he suggests is private money, but he outlines the impracticality of that approach due to economic reality and disincentives built into the system. The second possibility he offers is alternative currency brought forth by the federal government but dismisses that stating, "In the present political climate, the likelihood that any such arrangement will be made is essentially nil."[407]

The third possibility receives the bulk of his attention as well as his strong endorsement. He cites Supreme Court cases such as *Nebbia v. New York* (1934):

> *The States' "jurisdiction"—that is their legal authority—to employ gold and silver coin as alternative currencies is a "subject . . .which is not surrendered to the federal government." Rather, the Constitution explicitly reserves that power to the States.*[408]

He goes on to state that the Congress has no authority in this regard, boldly stating that the State right is "absolute."

> *The States enjoy a right and power to "make . . .gold and silver Coin a Tender" no matter what Congress may decree in the monetary field.*[409]

406. https://www.cato.org/sites/cato.org/files/serials/files/cato-journal/2015/5/cj-v35n2-3.pdf, page 210
407. Ibid, page 213
408. Ibid, page 215
409. Ibid, page 217

Vieira backed his argument with multiple Court ruling citations including *Lane County v. Oregon* (1869), *Julliard v. Greenman* (1884), *Taub v. Kentucky* (1988), and several others.

Amazingly, what he describes as the best means of implementation lines up precisely with what we have been suggesting:

> *Facilitating the use of "gold and silver Coin [as] a Tender" by inter alia*
> *(i) creating a State depository which would establish and manage accounts in "Coin" for the State and her citizens, transfer ownership of gold and silver among these accounts (by such means as electronic assignments, debit-cards, and checks), and maintain appropriate accounting-records for depositors;*
> *(ii) providing businessmen in the State with the necessary computer-software and instructions to enable them to price their goods and services in terms of "gold and silver Coin";*
> *(iii) offering incentives to businessmen to encourage their customers to employ "gold and silver Coin [as] a Tender" in dealing with their businesses;*
> *(iv) simplifying the calculation and collection of State and local taxes by allowing (for example) transactions effected in gold and silver to be valued, and taxes on or related to those transactions to be paid, in gold and silver; and*
> *(v) collecting selected taxes, fees, and other public charges in "gold and silver Coin" as soon as practicable, so as to familiarize as many citizens as possible with the existence, operations, and advantages of the alternative currency system.*[410]

Beyond that, Vieira also makes the case for the use of bullion transacted electronically, exactly in line with our proposal!

410. Ibid, pages 221-222

Second, through the use of gold and silver in forms other than "Coin." Economically sound, constitutional, and honest alternative currencies consisting of gold and silver need not employ those metals only in the form of "Coin."

From a technological perspective, probably the best alternatives available today are so-called electronic gold and electronic silver currencies. Here, "electronic" refers to the method for recording and transferring legal title to specific amounts of gold or silver bullion actually held by an "electronic currency provider" in separate accounts for each depositor's use as money. Such "electronic" currencies offer numerous advantages both of and over gold and silver coins:

- *Security: The gold and silver are owned by the depositors themselves and not by the "electronic currency providers" that hold those deposits. The depositors are bailors of the specie, the "providers" bailees. (With a typical bank, conversely, a deposit becomes the property of the bank, with the depositor merely a general creditor of the bank for the value of his deposit.)*
- *Ubiquity: Anyone maintaining an account with an "electronic currency provider" can easily acquire gold and silver through the "provider" and then deal with anyone else holding such an account, anywhere in the world.*
- *Convenience: transactions in gold and silver can be effected with debit cards or like instruments, so that payment is had immediately; but the actual specie may never have to leave the "electronic currency providers'" vaults. (Transactions also can be effected on the basis of paper orders in the nature of checks and drafts, or actual physical delivery of gold or silver, if the parties so desire.)*

- *Flexibility: Transactions of very small and exact values can be made—down to thousandths of a grain or a gram, or even less—which is impossible with coins.*
- *Accuracy: Details can be automatically recorded for purposes of accounting, including inter alia the date, the time, and the parties to a transaction; the location, nature, and purpose of the transaction; and its value in gold, silver, Federal Reserve Notes, or any other common media of exchange.*[411]

Vieira also shares a view very much in line with what I've been dreaming of for half a century.

> *To implement such a system, a State would establish within her government an official "electronic gold and silver currency provider." This agency might develop its own "electronic currency," or license the necessary technology from some private vendor…*
>
> *Particular depositors' gold and silver would be held in separate bailment accounts, so that the system could not be accused of operating on the basis of fractional reserves. This is critically important, inasmuch as any scheme utilizing "fractional reserves" would also necessarily implicate "Bills of Credit"—for if the State purported to credit a depositor's account with amounts of gold or silver bullion not owned by him, or not immediately subject to his order (either because they were not physically in the depository or were somehow legally encumbered), then those credits would amount at best to promises by the State to pay those amounts upon the depositor's demand at some future time, which is the essence of a "Bill of Credit" that functions as currency (Craig v. Missouri, 29 U.S. 410, 431-2 [1830]). Yet the depositors' gold and silver would always be impressed with the attributes of the State's sovereign authority, because the State had designated the metals as her own alternative currencies (Ling Su Fan v. United States, 218 U.S.302, 311 [1910], and Norman v. Baltimore & Ohio Railroad Co., 294 U.S. 240, 304 [1935]).*

411. Ibid, pages 222-223

> *Thus, the gold and silver in the State's depository would be serving, not only the particular purposes of the various depositors, both public and private, but also the overarching public purpose of guaranteeing the State's economic "homeland security." Consequently, not only the gold and silver deposited by the State and all of the governmental bodies and agencies within her jurisdiction, but also the specie deposited by members of her militia in their capacities and pursuant to their duties as such—which would include essentially all of her adult population—would be protected by an intergovernmental immunity, arising out of federalism itself, from any form of interference on the part of rogue agents of the General Government . . .*
>
> *Third, the constitutional equivalency of "Coin" and "electronic" currencies. The distinction between "electronic" gold and silver currencies, on the one hand, and actual "gold and silver Coin," on the other, is small in practice and inconsequential in principle. Instructive in this regard is the Supreme Court's decision in* Bronson v. Rodes *(74 U.S. 229 [1869]).*[412]

Finally, in listing ten advantages of such a system (well worth reading), Vieira answers one of the questions in advantage #7 that came up frequently when we proposed the notion in Texas.

> *...introduction of alternative gold and silver currencies would not depend upon a State's having any gold or silver in her treasury at the beginning of the process.*[413]

It is important to understand that in this proposal, the State does not have to have any gold or silver on deposit. The deposits belong to the individuals who placed them there. That is why the State is NOT coining money. The money belongs solely to the depositors. And the deposits can be in the form of bullion or for simplicity, the depositors can present traditional money and request that the Depository buy

412. Ibid, pages 223-225
413. Ibid, page 230

gold and silver with it to be held at the Depository. The State can charge to make purchases and sales, to conduct transactions, and also to hold the precious metal. The system is optional to citizens, but, as legal tender, can be forced into the financial system by the State. Banks and credit cards would have to accept gold and silver as legal tender, especially if it can be instantly exchanged into Federal Reserve money as an option. But then again, merchants might just prefer to keep the gold and silver!

NOTE:

The Bank for International Settlements (BIS) more or less through logical conclusion endorses the concept of electronic forms of gold and silver in their 2023 Blueprint for the future monetary system: improving the old, enabling the new report. Unfortunately, the BIS report goes on to endorse fully-programmable CBDC, a serious threat to our freedom!

> *The rapid expansion of trade and commerce over the past 500 years would be scarcely imaginable if buyers and sellers still had to cart around heavy chests full of metal coins to pay for goods and services. The advent of money in the form of book entries on ledgers overseen by trusted intermediaries opened the door to new financial instruments that bridged both geographical distance and the long lags between the delivery of goods and settlement of payments. With the advent of the electronic age, paper ledgers became digital, adding impetus to the "dematerialisation" of money as well as claims on financial and real assets. Electronic bookkeeping accelerated paper-based processes, allowing accounts to be updated at the speed of light.*[414]

414. https://www.bis.org/publ/arpdf/ar2023e3.htm

Vieira concludes his article with a passionate plea to adopt essentially what we have been promoting. He makes the case that this proposal is the best solution to the pending economic and political crisis.

> *If this can be accomplished, then for the first time in generations Americans will enjoy honest weights and measures in the monetary field—and with that reform, will have a realistic hope to restore honest commerce and even honest politics as well.*[415]

Isn't that worth the effort? Honest weights and measures![416] **This is the Founder's Pirate Money Secret, slipped into the Constitution, for such a time as this. Two centuries of Court rulings support it. Now, we have the technology to actuate it. And now, more than ever, we need it.**

Enough of the Constitutional history lesson. The point was to prove beyond any shadow of doubt that what we are proposing is not only legal but embodies the original intent of the Founders. It is 100% backed by Supreme Court rulings and is infinitely superior to the mess we have. Now, let's deal with the practical. In the final two chapters, we will dive deeper into how this will work, the benefits it will bring, and how you can help bring it about.

Told you things would look up!

415. https://www.cato.org/sites/cato.org/files/serials/files/cato-journal/2015/5/cj-v35n2-3.pdf, page 232
416. https://www.bible.com/bible/compare/PRO.20.23

GOLD CERTIFICATE FROM 1934

GOLD CERTIFICATE FROM 1928

Images: *National Numismatic Collection, National Museum of American History, Smithsonian Institution.*

I think the first duty of society is justice.
—Alexander Hamilton

8

Economic Justice

Let's face it. The wealth gap has widened sharply in the last 50 years and that is a serious problem. If you know me, you know that I don't make that statement lightly and it is certainly not an attack on free-market economics or capitalism. It's a fact, though, and evidence of economic injustice.[417]

But what is the cause? We believe it is unjust weights and measures (something God hates according to the Bible).[418] Using the Monopoly analogy, someone has stacked the *Community Chest* and *Chance* decks and is now controlling the bank. When we left sound money, the economy became untethered, and speculators took advantage through financialization using fiat money. The rich got richer while the middle class shrank.

417. https://www.ipsos.com/en-us/most-americans-think-economy-rigged-rich-and-powerful
418. https://www.bible.com/bible/compare/PRO.20.23

This is why we must provide a path back to Economic Justice! It starts with just weights and measures available to everyone, not just the wealthy! This can be made possible, according to monetary expert Edwin Vieira, Jr. if we return to Gold and Silver as money.[419] This will pave the way for Economic Justice!

Let's review the evidence starting with some quotes from academic studies cited in *Global Times*:

> *Since the 1970s, income inequality and wealth disparity in the United States have continually deepened. The rich keep getting richer, the poor keep getting poorer, and the middle class is squeezed. Today, these perilous trends continue . . .*
>
> *The middle class is shrinking. A "middle-class America" was formed in some 20 years from the end of World War II to 1970. Afterward, however, despite the continued growth of the U.S. economy, the middle class has not expanded, but shrunk significantly. The share of American adults who live in middle-income households fell from 61 percent in 1971 to 51 percent in 2019. The share in the upper-income tier rose from 14 percent to 20 percent over the same period. Meanwhile, the share in the lower-income tier increased from 25 percent to 29 percent. The size of middle-income families has continued to shrink.*[420]

While *Global Times* gets the outcome right, they miss the actual cause, blaming partisanship, racial inequity, and the institution of capitalism. While those may have had some impact, their own data clearly shows a growing middle class from 1945 until the early 1970s. Was race truly less of a problem before the Civil Rights movement? Did we abandon capitalism in 1945 just to pick it back up in 1970? Of course not. Yet the data is clear. The middle class was growing

419. https://www.cato.org/sites/cato.org/files/serials/files/cato-journal/2015/5/cj-v35n2-3.pdf page 232
420. https://www.globaltimes.cn/page/202302/1286098.shtml

coming out of the war and then started declining about 50 years ago. What changed?

Obviously, there are many factors at work.[421] One huge one and maybe the most important factor, too often overlooked, was the total rejection of sound money for purely fiat currency in 1971 under Nixon.[422] That was a Monopoly board flip that put bankers in charge of everything. It was the start of the "financialization" of our economy, the source of the rich getting richer. Before 1971, America got wealthy by making things. Over the past 50 years, however, the primary path to wealth has been making money with money, the very definition of financialization.[423] But let's be clear. Abandoning the last vestiges of the gold standard is what opened the door to financialization.

> *The beginnings of financialization in the United States can be traced back to the 1950s. However, the financial sector didn't expand until much later in the 20th century, especially after the collapse of the Bretton Woods system . . .**
>
> *[Author's note: Bretton Woods fell when Nixon closed the gold window in 1971.[424]]
>
> *The Bretton Woods agreement—which tied international currencies to the US dollar and anchored the dollar to gold—created predictable exchange rates and limited speculation. Thus, when this fell, a new period marked by free trade and the free movement of capital began. This also created instability in the global markets from which the financial industry has profited.*[425]

421. https://www.zerohedge.com/markets/how-bidenomics-generates-more-debt-and-inflation
422. https://www.theblaze.com/op-ed/roth-blame-government-for-the-reason-young-adults-are-still-living-with-their-parents
423. https://www.industryweek.com/the-economy/public-policy/article/21252236/how-the-financialization-of-america-hurt-workers-and-the-economy
424. https://youtu.be/iRzr1QU6K1o?t=61
425. https://www.investopedia.com/terms/f/financialization.asp

What is Financialization and How Has It Hurt Us?

> *Financialism is totally about making money from money and has nothing to do with creating jobs or shared prosperity . . .*
>
> *It is no coincidence that the rise of financialization has happened during the decline of manufacturing, middle-class income and capital investment, and the rise of inequality. It is also no coincidence that during the same period there was an enormous shift in wealth to the top 10% earners at the expense of the bottom 90 . . .*
>
> *Financialization is about risky trading and the return on net assets that benefits its shareholders but not the parts of the economy that could lead to long-term growth. Financialization is not a good long-term strategy for manufacturing or the economy. The financial sector used to be the servant of business, which funneled money into productive enterprises. Today they are the masters who dictate to business. They are creating a debt bubble that could lead to another financial collapse and bailout. We ignore it at our peril.*[426]

OK. Sharing those truths will make me few friends on Wall Street, the mecca of my chosen profession. But I'm not about making money here. Rather, we are about saving America!

I was the University of Tulsa's candidate and a state finalist for a Rhodes Scholarship in 1983. My answer to one of the questions probably cost me the chance for a degree from Oxford. But I was unwilling to buy into financialization and globalism. Even getting hired by the venerable Templeton organization in the 1990s didn't change my perspective. The goal of life should not be about making money at the expense of others. Yet that is precisely what financialization does.

426. https://www.industryweek.com/the-economy/public-policy/article/21252236/how-the-financialization-of-america-hurt-workers-and-the-economy

The Solution for Economic Justice

If ending the gold standard created the environment for the problem, it stands to reason that returning to a sound money system must be part of the solution. Remember the quote from Thomas Jefferson at the top of Chapter Six (*Paper is poverty. It is only the ghost of money, and not money itself.*)? Or the quote from J.P. Morgan at the top of Chapter Seven (*Gold is money. Everything else is credit.*)? This is true at the societal level but also very true for individuals. Paper is credit for the wealthy but poverty for everyone else. Only those with means can access real money like gold and silver. Let me explain.

Remember when I shared in Chapter Seven about my client who passed away with three rolls of gold coins in her safe? Her estate took weeks to locate, value, liquidate, and get paid for them. It was terribly inefficient. She was a wealthy woman (and a real sweetheart) who also owned stocks, bonds, and real estate. Her most solid holding was likely the gold, but it was also the most difficult in a practical sense. That got me to thinking. How could someone of limited means ever afford to have money tied up in gold?

Imagine you have worked hard and saved up an extra $1,000. What do you do with it? Do you buy stocks? No way because you might need the money in an emergency and your stock might be down. Most people in that circumstance would hold cash or put it in the bank. Most wouldn't buy any gold or silver, not knowing how or where to buy it safely. They most certainly couldn't wait weeks to liquidate if an emergency like plumbing repairs rose.

And yet, despite this, people are looking to buy gold. They just don't know how. Did you know that "How to Buy Gold" became a top Google search term in 2023 according to a recent article in *The Wall Street Journal*?

'How to Buy Gold' Hits a Google Record as Crypto Investors Chase World's Oldest Asset

The old-school precious metal has new allure for a generation seeking a respite from the cryptocurrency roller coaster[427]

The point of the article is that people are desperate for a monetary alternative to the paper dollar. They rushed to bitcoin only to discover the government attacking it. They fear CBDC. So where to turn? Gold and silver are increasingly their answer according to *The Wall Street Journal* (emphasis added to highlight key points):

> *For three years, Mitch Day rode bitcoin's wild swings, through the record highs of 2021 to the cold-water plunge of 2022. Mr. Day and a number of his cryptocurrency compatriots have since turned to* ***the asset favored by*** *pharaohs,* ***pirates****, and Scrooge McDuck, helping drive an outbreak of gold fever.*
>
> *"For a long time, I kind of figured,* ***'Oh gold and silver?' That's kind of the old guy-thing,"*** *said Mr. Day, a 27-year-old college student in Kelowna, British Columbia. "Sure, I'm not necessarily going to get rich buying gold, but it will hold that money in uncertain times better than a lot of other things." . . .*
>
> ***Google searches for the phrase "how to buy gold" have hit their highest recorded level so far this month, according to Google Trends data going back about two decades*** *. . .*
>
> *Gold was prized by ancient Egyptians and Incans. It lured European explorers to the New World and the original 49ers to California. The precious metal remains a staple in investors' portfolios,* ***prized for its stability and as a hedge against inflation*** *. . .*

427. https://www.wsj.com/articles/weary-bitcoin-investors-chase-shiny-new-objectgold-21f8a6ee

> *Mr. Day knows gold isn't going to take him to the moon, echoing the lingo of traders who believe a particular cryptocurrency will skyrocket in value. He buys gold coins to preserve his wealth. Bitcoin shares common qualities with gold: Both are mined.* ***Neither is wallet friendly. And they are virtually useless for buying gas, groceries, or a movie ticket.***[428]

Truth is that the wealthy have lots of ways to beat inflation. They can afford to hide in bitcoin. Or hold gold and silver. Or own private equity, venture capital, or derivatives. But ordinary people don't buy bitcoin. And they can't put short-term savings in risky investments. Gold and silver don't work because, as *The Wall Street Journal* explains, **they are not "...wallet friendly. And they are virtually useless for buying gas, groceries, or a movie ticket."**

And there is the point. Economic justice can be achieved with sound money (gold and silver), but sound money has not been wallet friendly and thus is inaccessible. People are searching Google for answers to this dilemma.

Good News! Modern Pirate Money Works for Everyone!

As we've explained, a state (like Texas or really any state) can establish a bullion depository and declare gold and silver as legal tender using the authority granted by the United States Constitution. It can buy gold and silver for depositors, make it transactional (through a debit card), keep records, and sell gold and silver when depositors want to cash out. The technology exists and works today. Because the holdings are legal tender, they may not be subject to capital gains tax even if they hold their value during inflation.

The middle class would have a simple way to buy, sell, and transact in gold and silver. They would have an optional gold or silver

428. Ibid

standard to join with at least a part of their assets. The downsides of illiquidity, cap gains tax, storage costs, and just the complexity of learning how to buy and sell could be vanquished. All the upside of gold doubloons and silver pieces of eight with none of the headaches thanks to modern technology.

You may have a bazillion questions at this point about the practicality of how this could work. In the next chapter we will lay out the steps needed to bring this off the drawing board and into the real world. But before we get there, let's consider the FAQs we encountered when promoting two companion bills in the 88th Texas Legislature, one in the Senate and an identical version in the House. These bills were designed to do exactly what I've been describing. As we met with legislators and spoke to groups across Texas, we got a lot of questions. We then summarized those and put them on a website.

The following FAQ section is taken from https://www.transactionalgold.com/:

WHAT IS THIS AGAIN? WHY AM I LOOKING AT THIS? (SHORT ANSWER)

These bills should allow any citizen, business, or legal entity to utilize our Texas Bullion Depository (TBD) to buy, sell, or store their own gold and silver. By using existing debit card technology, your constituents can make everyday purchases or pay bills with gold and silver. Everyone can participate if they desire. (Left, Right, Center, Wealthy, or not!) Texas would earn standard fees already paid by merchants. Other states are interested! Participation is optional. It is just another safe, secure way to pay!

WHY IS THIS IMPORTANT?

Gold and silver have been a stable source of currency for centuries. They are the fairest form of money. Inflation is hurting many these days, and they are looking for solutions. This is the answer. This is your opportunity to help bring Wall Street-level diversification to everyday Americans.

SB2334 and HB4903 give the authority to the Comptroller of Texas to monetize and democratize the owning and spending of gold and silver, helping people preserve their buying power.]

IS THIS A BRAND-NEW CONCEPT? HAS IT BEEN DONE BEFORE?

This is not a new concept and is being done right now in a variety of commercial applications. Most require gold to help in Switzerland. We think it would be great for Texans to have their gold in Texas! You can also see a one-minute explainer video[429] to see how it works. Bringing it to Texas offers both practical and legal advantages.

ISN'T THIS JUST ANOTHER CRYPTO OR DIGITAL CURRENCY WITH ALL ITS COMPLICATIONS?

NO, this is not a crypto at all, and it is not actually digital any more than a debit card is digital. It is electronic just like what we all use already.

IS THIS EQUITABLE OR JUST ANOTHER WAY FOR THE RICH TO GET RICHER? HOW CAN THE AVERAGE PERSON USE IT WHEN THEY CANNOT AFFORD TO GET IN?

429. https://youtu.be/X7xisUdUzoY

Every American, regardless of economic class, deserves the option to have money held in precious metals as a protection against inflation. Now they can hold gold and silver and spend it when needed! Anyone who can afford a checking account will be able to "get in." We've seen the success of commercial versions such as GlintPay and they have very low minimums, sometimes below the minimum required for a checking account.

IS IT COMPLICATED TO DO?

NO, anyone who wants to participate can do so by simply opening an account at the TBD. It would be similar to opening a bank account.

HOW CAN YOU COMPETE WITH CREDIT CARDS THAT GIVE MILES, POINTS, 30 DAYS CASH FLOW, PAYMENT OPTIONS, ETC.?

The intention is not to compete with credit cards. This is a debit card. However, there are many advantages to gold-based money including potential inflation protection. Individuals can still use their credit cards if they'd like. But when it comes time to pay the credit card bill, they could pay it with gold and silver holdings rather than from their traditional checking account. That way they get both the perks and the security of having gold- and silver-based money in Texas.

THIS SEEMS TOO GOOD TO BE TRUE. WHAT IS THE CATCH? IS THERE SOME ORGANIZATION THAT IS PUSHING THIS TO MAKE PRIVATE MONEY ON IT?

No catch. Those who benefit financially from this Bill are people from every economic status AND the state of Texas. The state can make significant revenue from transaction fees - already paid by merchants, storage, and conversion fees. The Texans seeking passage of this bill want to see all Texans benefit.

WHAT IF DEPOSITORS WANT PHYSICAL POSSESSION OF THEIR OWN GOLD?

Simple. They can remove it anytime they want from the TBD. They can either come and pick it up or withdraw their balance by converting back to US Dollars.

WHAT KIND OF THINGS CAN YOU PURCHASE WITH THIS NEW INSTRUMENT OF THE TBD, THIS NEW WAY TO PAY?

Because Texas is such an important state, 9th largest economy in the world, this is a way to pay anywhere in the world. The credit card companies will convert it on the fly just as they do Dollars, Pounds, and Euros. TBD debit card holders could pay bills, buy coffee, entertainment, travel. You name it!

Merchants will be able to accept this form of payment, as they do now with other debit and credit cards.

IS THIS MAKING TEXAS INTO A BANK?

NO. This would just be another monetary service. Texas already has a depository for gold. Adding a debit card technology on top simply provides people functional access to it. The depository will be able to offer Texas-based money (actually gold and silver) and work with banks. The depository will not offer the wide array of services that banks currently offer. Furthermore, Texas banks could offer either "paper accounts" based on the US dollar or gold and silver accounts (based on Texas Transactional Currency). We believe many banks will want to offer both.

DOES THIS MEAN THAT TEXAS NEEDS TO BUY GOLD TO BACK THIS CURRENCY?

NO, Texas will NOT own the gold or silver that is this currency. These bills provide for purchases and sales on the open market through the depository rather than from reserves held in the depository. This will be gold and silver owned by the individual, business, or legal entity. The value of the gold and silver a person has on deposit is the amount they can spend via their TBD debit card.

WILL THERE BE TAX IMPLICATIONS?

Upon passage, be sure to check with a professional tax advisor or accountant to determine any tax implications. We believe there may not be capital gains or losses when using gold as tender.

For many, it will be the first time they have had access to gold and the easy ability to spend it. SB2334 and HB4903 makes gold function as tender. Gold then can easily be transactional allowing your constituents and everyone else who wants it to have all the benefits of owning gold and at the same time have a great way to make secure payments.

IS THIS LEGAL?

YES! Using gold and silver is a State Right secured in the U.S. Constitution Article 1, Section 10. The Texas Bullion Depository is already authorized by TX Gov. Code Sec. 2116 which has numerous supportive provisions (https://statutes.capitol.texas.gov/Docs/GV/htm/GV.2116.htm). There are several US Supreme Court rulings that support this state right.

I DON'T KNOW ANYTHING ABOUT THE TEXAS BULLION DEPOSITORY, WHAT CAN YOU TELL ME?

A lot! But you can learn more at www.texasbulliondepository.gov.

IS THE GOLD SAFE AND /OR INSURED AT THE TEXAS BULLION DEPOSITORY?

YES, the TBD is currently insured by Lloyd's of London. But don't take our word for it! You can learn more at https://www.texasbulliondepository.gov/faqs.

WHAT IF THE PRICE OF GOLD GOES DOWN?

It is true that gold prices fluctuate and there is a risk of lost purchasing power when you own gold. People should keep that in mind when converting to a gold- or silver-based currency. But throughout history, gold and silver have never been worth zero. Further, the US dollar also has risks and fluctuates relative to other currencies as well as goods and services. We feel it beneficial to have the opportunity to have transactional gold and silver in addition to paper money.

Without this plan, we will face continuing Economic Injustice and an increasing wealth gap. Financialization will continue unabated. The middle class will be forced to rely on cash in the form of fiat money, a depreciating asset soon to be under serious attack.[430] **If we do nothing, programmable CBDC will be forced upon us with no means of escape. The villain of the story is unsound money. The solution is Modern Pirate Money.**

Let's learn how we can together make this happen. Let's bring Economic Justice! Let's be pirates! Arghhhh!

430. https://www.activistpost.com/2023/05/americans-say-families-need-85000-to-get-by-up-from-58000-in-2013.html

Let's roll!
—Todd Beamer

9

Traveling the Yellow Brick Road with Silver Slippers

There was a time when I was very young (maybe 4 or 5) that I really did not like *The Wizard of Oz*. No, it wasn't that I thought it was lame. It scared me. It wasn't the Tin Man, the Lion, the Scarecrow, or the witches. Or the munchkins. Or even the Wizard. What scared me was the tornado. I never got past the very beginning.

Keep in mind that I grew up in Oklahoma and tornadoes made almost nightly appearances in the spring.[431] The National Weather Service would interrupt television with watches and warnings and sirens. Sometimes we'd see pictures of the aftermath on the news or in the paper. Everyone talked about it. And then, right there in

431. https://data.oklahoman.com/tornado-archive/oklahoma/1966/

black and white on the TV screen (and yes, even though the movie starts in black and white, I don't think we had a color TV yet) was a "real tornado," or at least it looked like one to me.[432] It did big damage, destroying the farm and whisking poor Dorothy and Toto in the farmhouse far away from Kansas.[433]

You may be wondering what in the world my irrational childhood fear of a movie has to do with what we are talking about. The truth is that because I hated tornadoes, I refused to watch *The Wonderful Wizard of Oz*. And because I hated the movie, I refused to read the book. As a result, I missed out on what I later learned may have been a commentary on monetary systems.[434] That was the kind of thing I loved to read in first grade (along with *Treasure Island* of course). Except the tornado scared me away.

While some scholars disagree, there certainly is a case to be made that the book (more than the movie) is about gold and silver as money. Hugh Rockoff, an economist, wrote a 1990 article, "The 'Wizard of Oz' as a Monetary Allegory," published in the prestigious *Journal of Political Economy*.[435] He explains that the author of the book, L. Frank Baum, was writing at a point of intense monetary debate. And it is true that many of the characters and elements resemble those involved in that debate. For example, "the yellow brick road" could reference gold. Dorothy's shoes were silver in the book, not ruby slippers (MGM changed them to show off the power of technicolor). The city, Oz, happens to be the abbreviation for ounce. Supposedly,

432. https://en.wikipedia.org/wiki/The_Wizard_of_Oz_on_television
433. https://youtu.be/RQWSh7Db-_E
434. https://lawliberty.org/the-wizard-of-oz-as-an-allegory-for-the-1896-presidential-election/
435. https://www.jstor.org/stable/pdf/2937766.pdf

the Scarecrow represents western farmers while the Tin Man represents factory workers. The munchkins? People in the Northeast under the control of bankers. The Emerald City? Green just like fiat paper money led by an impotent wizard with nothing powerful behind the curtain. Read this way, to get Dorothy home required following the yellow brick road but only with silver slippers. In other words, a combination of gold and silver as money.[436]

I share this uncertain as to whether Baum's book was intended to be an "economic fairy tale." One thing is clear. The year he wrote it, 1900, was a period of hot debate over what should constitute money. And all the factions (farmers, workers in industry, politicians, bankers, and even ordinary citizens) were educated on the role of money and the form it should take. Over the past century and a quarter, however, our population has been dumbed down and that is to our detriment. We are facing a potential tornado of destruction and a variety of threats and yet people are largely ignorant. Worse than ignorant, they are complacent. In Baum's day, there were great debates. Should America be on a gold standard or a gold and silver standard? This was actually part of the presidential race of 1896.[437] Today, people argue over stupid tweets.

That is the purpose of this book. To get Americans educated and help them find their way home. Otherwise, we will be hit by a debt tornado, a de-dollarize/de-Americanize the world tornado, and a Great Reset/CBDC tornado all leading to a dystopian nightmare. We won't be in Kansas, anymore, or any part of America for that matter. Instead, we will be trapped in a strange land with wicked witches and flying monkeys, and all the worst of *Animal Farm*, *1984*, and *Brave New World* rolled into one real-life horror movie. Now that really does scare me!

---

436. https://www.yahoo.com/entertainment/video/heres-real-forgotten-meaning-wizard-040000330.html
437. https://www.britannica.com/event/United-States-presidential-election-of-1896

Seven Steps to Solving the Money Problem

So how do we fix it? We know the solution was laid out in the Constitution. We are talking modern pirate money (both gold and silver) made convenient through technology, legalized as tender by a state. Private, but also optional. Let's be clear on that. This is not a proposal to replace the Federal Reserve. Rather, it is a plan to give people an option with their money if they choose.

Here are the seven steps necessary to implement the plan:

1. **Get educated.**
   If you've read this book, you already know more than 99.9% of Americans about the history of money, what the Constitution says about money, and the economic impacts of money. Plus, you have access to more than 400 footnotes as opportunities for further reading and study. These represent the best thinking on the subject from the past three centuries. Counting the Biblical references, you have access to wisdom on money from most of recorded history.

2. **Identify like-minded supporters, legislators, and elected officials.**
   Next, start spreading the word. Find the tea parties and political groups that would show interest. Tea parties were formed because we were spending too much money and headed toward the fiscal cliff.[438] This was on the heels of a massive $789 billion Obama-led economic stimulus package and then another $75 billion proposal to pay the mortgages of distressed homeowners.[439,440,441] That makes tea parties ideal locations to find like-minded allies. But do not stop

438. https://claremontreviewofbooks.com/the-meaning-of-the-tea-party/
439. https://www.nytimes.com/2009/02/12/us/politics/12stimulus.html
440. https://www.thedailybeast.com/when-cnbc-created-the-tea-party
441. https://washingtonmonthly.com/2021/02/19/the-tea-party-began-12-years-ago-whats-changed-and-what-hasnt/

there! Tea parties tend to be Republican, but we discovered that many Democrats like the Economic Justice our plan provides, especially since it is a choice rather than a mandate. Young people love bitcoin and worry about the dollar. Look for allies across the spectrum. Share this book or point people to the *Economic War Room*® (www.economicwarroom.com).

One of your goals should be to find a legislator or two that would take up the banner. The cleanest way to actualize this opportunity is in state legislation. We can help with that as I am speaking to both the legislators and state financial officers (such as state comptrollers and treasurers) on a regular basis. We have started a list and crafted some model legislation to make it easy to begin (see Appendix A). In addition, we are educating pastors and financial advisors regarding the merit of this approach. This is a matter of Biblical justice (honest weights and measures) and provides a good option for clients worried about inflation and other economic challenges.

NOTE:

To get an idea of where your state may stand on these issues, check out Is Your State Protecting Financial Freedom? at CoreysDigs. It includes "tools to track state legislation related to precious metals, cryptocurrencies, and by using a 'Full Text Search' of bills in each state."[442]

442. https://www.coreysdigs.com/solutions/is-your-state-protecting-financial-freedom-get-the-full-breakdown-here/

If you have access to your governor, get her or him a copy of this book. Likewise, seek out friendly media to see if they would consider writing a story. Our intention is to build a movement. Our hub is www.transactionalgold.com and as we advance, we will add resources there.

3. **Explain, Encourage, Engage.**
   Not everyone you meet will be willing to read a book, even one as fun, entertaining, and well-written as this one. [Oh, and I forgot to mention humble. :)] So, you should be prepared to explain the how and why of it as simply as possible.

   For most people, you may not want to get into the depths of monetary history. Rather, you will want to focus on how this is just "another way to pay" for stuff. Convenient. Simple. And an easy way to own gold and silver. The tax benefits are appealing. Also, the idea that you won't have to worry about a run on the bank since the gold and silver held there belong to you. For some, privacy will be the big deal. For others, it may be that they won't be cancelled or have their spending controlled. The fact is that almost everyone will find one or more reasons to like this. You just have to find the hot button that works. We will put some one-page flyers you can download, print, and use at www.transactionalgold.com (subject to terms of use).

4. **Work the bill with an action plan.**
   One thing that will motivate a state representative or senator is knowing that there is a grassroots community in favor and willing to work. We had great success in Texas. When we started, we were told that there was zero chance we would even get a hearing. We shocked everyone when a core group of several dozen people jumped on multiple conference calls a week, began a phone bank, and regularly traveled to Austin.

These are real heroes and included in the group are some of the top conservative leaders in America today. Please see my list of acknowledgments at the end of the book.

Our action plan included seven critical elements: 1) letters to the Governor, Lieutenant Governor, House Speaker, and committee leadership from people they know (like major donors) or would recognize. 2) a celebrity petition signed by recognizable people who believe in economic justice. 3) groups of supporters willing to walk the halls of the capitol and meet with legislators and staff. 4) creative marketing such as the passing out of foil-wrapped chocolate coins and the printing of faux debit cards. 5) strategic media placed and shared with key leadership. 6) a website with key marketing themes. 7) an AlignAct campaign[443] and a text/phone call campaign targeting the legislators individually.

NOTE:

My beautiful and brilliant wife Marnie had the suggestion that we pass out gold- and silver-wrapped chocolate coins in every legislative office we visited. We stopped at the local Party City and bought out their stock, packaging bags of coins to give along with a faux debit card. For the legislators, we printed personalized cards.

Later we learned the meaning and significance of giving chocolate coins, known in the Jewish community as Gelt. This is a tradition that goes back to the origins of Hanukkah as explained by Rabbi Deborah R. Prinz:

Gelt refers to chocolate coins given to Jewish children on the festival of Hanukkah. They are usually wrapped in gold foil, and their history can be traced back to the decision of the Hasmoneans to mint

443. https://alignact.com/go/texas-transactional-gold---next-steps---special-session

NOTE:

their own nation's coins after their military victory over the Greek Syrians. Gelt is often used to gamble with in the game of dreidel.

The gelt of Hanukkah recalls the booty, including coins, that the Maccabean victors distributed to the Jewish widows, soldiers, and orphans, possibly at the first celebration of the rededication of the Jerusalem Temple. Also, in ancient Israel, striking, minting, and distributing coins expressed Hanukkah's message of political autonomy.[444]

We didn't realize the spiritual significance of giving those coins. In essence, we were celebrating in advance the importance of state-based gold and silver money as a symbol of freedom, just like the Maccabees more than 2,000 years ago.

444. https://reformjudaism.org/learning/answers-jewish-questions/what-story-behind-hanukkah-gelt

5. **Help us build a compact of states.**
   Texas, on a stand-alone basis, would be perhaps the ninth largest economy in the world and maybe soon the eighth.[445] On its own, Texas with $2.1 trillion in GDP has a larger economy than Canada, Mexico, South Korea, and Russia and is roughly on par with Italy. In fact, on a relative basis, Texas is a bigger part of the global economy than China was at the turn of the century. Why shouldn't Texas have its own money?

   But Texas alone is not nearly as strong as it would be with Oklahoma, Florida, South Carolina, Virginia, Kansas, Alaska, Arkansas, Tennessee, and Arizona. Those are just a few of the other states expressing interest in transactional gold and silver. Combined they have an economy approaching $6 trillion in GDP.[446] That would place these 10 states third in world rankings, only behind the U.S. and China, but ahead of Japan, Germany, the United Kingdom, France, and India.[447]

   If Texas and any combination of those other nine interested states moved forward with our plan, it would be unstoppable![448] And the best part about it is that only simple state legislation is required. The Constitutional right is clear, and the technology is available. Plus, all the states could launch with the existing Texas Bullion Depository for speed to market. In fact, once one state has implemented the idea, other states could simply declare that state's money as legal tender. There are multiple ways to make it happen. **The key point? This is very doable!**

445. https://www.statesman.com/story/opinion/columns/guest/2023/04/07/business-incentives-help-keep-texas-economy-strong/70088933007/
446. https://wisevoter.com/state-rankings/gdp-by-state/
447. https://worldpopulationreview.com/countries/by-gdp
448. https://centerforsecuritypolicy.org/states-protect-america-from-foreign-adversaries/

6. **After the legislation is passed, we must work together to save the nation.**

   One thing we learned quickly is that when you bring out a big idea like this one, some people get greedy. I can't tell you how many people showed up or called demanding we adopt their technology or hire them to make this happen. Many people were looking for their "piece of the action." That is not to say we won't need technology. And some of the people showed up sincerely with good ideas, great suggestions, and worthy contacts for helpful tech. But everyone needs to understand the process from idea to implementation. There's no need for technology until the legislation is passed.

   Fortunately, we have a "proof of concept" already in place with Glint and other gold-based debit cards. We also have the Texas Bullion Depository (TBD) that is up and operating. Essentially, what we need to do is marry those two and add silver to the mix. Not saying it's simple. But I am saying that the proof of concept is in place. How a state wants to implement the idea will likely be left to their Comptroller or Treasurer. There will be a vendor bidding process to either build the system or to integrate the technology. And states will need marketing teams to encourage adoption. There will be plenty of opportunities for entrepreneurs to build, grow, and profit from or around transactional gold and silver money. It's just imperative that the steps are done in the proper order and with the right heart. We cannot allow this powerful initiative to be derailed by greed, corruption, or incompetence.

   We need the best and brightest to come together with sincere hearts to make this happen. Think of the early patriots willing to sacrifice lives, fortunes, and sacred honor to birth America. We have an amazing opportunity today to do something very meaningful. Who can question that we are here, now, for such a time as this?[449]

7. **Finally, I would urge everyone to pray fervently for this to come to pass. If you are a believing Christian, you should understand several things:**
   a. *The Bible is clear that real money is gold and silver (and occasionally copper).*[450,451,452,453]
   b. *Fiat paper money is an unjust weight and measure, and God hates those.*[454,455,456]
   c. *Jesus taught in the parable of the talents that the master expects us to "conduct business until he returns."*[457,458] *If we get shut out of the money system either cancelled or via CBDC, we cannot fulfill that commandment.*[459]

This plan is very Biblical, providing economic justice to those who are less fortunate and opportunity for everyone. Therefore, we should bathe it in prayer, listening intently for the Holy Spirit, and obeying faithfully what we hear. The threats are not just economic, they are spiritual as well. Thus, our response must be both economic and spiritual!

For Christians, it is important to have the right perspective on money. I have another book coming out soon titled, *The Economic War of the Heart*. It will share three truths about silver and gold that must be

449. https://www.biblegateway.com/passage/?search=Esther%204%3A14&version=NIV
450. https://schiffgold.com/commentaries/bible-say-gold-silver
451. https://www.openbible.info/topics/gold_and_silver
452. https://atlantagoldandcoin.com/how-gold-silver-were-viewed-valued-used-in-biblical-times/
453. https://medium.com/@silverbullion/gold-and-silver-gods-money-in-the-bible-df2567fb0966
454. https://www.jeremiahproject.com/new-world-order/just-weights-measures/
455. https://publicpolicyinstitutewju.wordpress.com/2013/07/30/righteous-and-evil-money-what-christians-have-to-learn-from-the-bible-and-the-founders/
456. https://www.openbible.info/topics/honest_weight_and_measures
457. https://biblehub.com/luke/19-13.htm
458. https://bible.org/seriespage/lesson-88-doing-business-jesus-luke-1911-27
459. https://www.fulcrum7.com/blog/2022/5/27/the-christian-and-programmable-money-cbdcs

understood. 1) Silver and gold cannot save you. Money is a tool to be used. It is not a desire to obtain. Zephaniah 1:18 (paraphrased) declares, "*Your silver and gold won't save you at the day of the wrath of the Lord.*"[460] 2) Silver and gold may buy health care but God doesn't need them to heal you. Acts 3:6 (NKJV) explains, "*Silver and gold I do not have, but what I do have I give you: In the name of Jesus Christ of Nazareth, rise up and walk.*"[461] And 3) Ultimately, the silver and gold aren't yours anyway as explained in Haggai 2:8 (NKJV), "*The silver is mine, and the gold is mine, says the LORD of hosts.*"[462]

There is HOPE but we have no time to waste. Inflation (the loss of purchasing power) is just the tip of a very large iceberg and we, sadly, seem to be on the Titanic headed straight for it. China, Russia, and the BRICS nations see gold as their weapon to damage America. Global elitists and sell-out politicians see CBDC as a means to enslave us. Fortunately, the Founders gave us an amazing escape plan that can protect families, states, and ultimately the nation as a whole. It is modern "pirate money," transactional gold and silver made legal tender by the states.[463]

We have the plan. Let's Roll!

460. https://biblehub.com/zephaniah/1-18.htm
461. https://biblehub.com/acts/3-6.htm
462. https://biblehub.com/haggai/2-8.htm
463. https://discernreport.com/3-ways-physical-precious-metals-defend-against-the-central-bank-digital-currencies-around-the-corner/

SILVER CERTIFICATE FROM 1891

SILVER CERTIFICATE FROM 1923

Images: *National Numismatic Collection, National Museum of American History, Smithsonian Institution.*

PIRATE MONEY

AFTERWORD

Coming from Cherokee ancestry, the concept of Economic Justice is much more than a slogan. There was an inherent injustice in the way the Cherokee and other indigenous peoples were forced from their native lands, promised permanent territory "as long as the grass grows and the rivers run," and then having those treaties broken without recourse.[464] Even the pejorative of "Indian Giver" is misunderstood.[465] Because the Native peoples had little concept of money, they would exchange gifts in a form of barter. If I give you something, it was only polite to return a gift of like value. But to the American settlers, this was viewed as rude. For my ancestors, however, the rude thing was taking their land, marching them on the Trail of Tears, promising a permanent homestead, and then taking even that back when oil was discovered! The book and new movie *Killers of the Flower Moon* provide a reasonable historical perspective on a major atrocity that happened very close to my birthplace just 100 years ago.[466]

464. https://savingplaces.org/stories/as-long-as-the-grass-grows-and-the-rivers-run-native-american-treaties-today
465. https://www.ictinc.ca/blog/indian-giver-can-we-give-it-back
466. https://www.davidgrann.com/book/killers-of-the-flower-moon/

Don't get me wrong, I LOVE AMERICA! However, this is a nation with flaws and faults. But overall, there is no better place to live. Most of the Native peoples I know feel similarly. **But it is way past time for genuine Economic Justice!** We are all being given what will soon amount to worthless paper in exchange for our hard work, goods, and services. And then, with CBDC, even that can be taken away if we aren't "good little Indians" or if we stray from "the Reservation." Feels like déjà-vu. **My native sensibilities cry out for Economic Justice.**

The beautiful thing is that the Founders of the United States provided a hidden plan that will work for all peoples, regardless of ancestry. It will protect us from a new taking by out-of-control politicians, elites, the World Economic Forum, and the Chinese Communist Party-led BRICS.

If you agree that "pirate money" is the answer to the multiple economic, financial, and monetary challenges we are facing, and you want true Economic Justice, please help us spread the word! This is the path forward for Liberty, Security, and Values in America. Not just for the wealthy but for everyone.

At PirateMoneyBook.com, you can order additional copies to share with friends and colleagues. Bulk orders for distribution to legislators can be made available. Use the camera on your smartphone to capture the QR code below.

We believe that this may be the most important financial message of the decade. It could save our nation and protect your family.

Join the movement. Spread the word!

APPENDIX A

Sample Legislation Proposed for Texas

By: ______________________________ H.B. No. __________

A BILL TO BE ENTITLED

AN ACT

relating to the establishment of a transactional currency based on gold and silver, authorizing a fee.

BE IT ENACTED BY THE LEGISLATURE OF THE STATE OF TEXAS:

SECTION 1. Subtitle A, Title 4, Government Code, is amended by adding Chapter 404A to read as follows:

CHAPTER 404A. GOLD AND SILVER CURRENCY

SUBCHAPTER A. GENERAL PROVISIONS

Sec. 404A.0001. DEFINITIONS. In this chapter:

(1) "Bullion" means precious metals as defined within the Government Code Chapter 2116 limited to gold and silver only.

(2) "Transactional currency" means a representation of actual gold and silver, specie and bullion held in a Depository account by a Depository account holder as defined within the Government Code Chapter 2116 and which may be transferred by electronic instruction. Such representation shall reflect the exact unit(s) of physical specie or gold and silver bullion in the pooled depository account in its fractional troy ounce measurement as provided by this chapter.

(3) "Precious metal" means precious metal as defined within the Government Code Chapter 2116 limited to gold and silver.

(4) "Pooled depository account" means the account in the Texas Bullion Depository established under Section 404A.0052.

(5) "Specie" means a precious metal stamped into coins as defined within the Government Code Chapter 2116.

Sec. 404A.0002. RULES. The comptroller may adopt rules as necessary or convenient to implement this chapter, including rules to:

(1) ensure the security of the specie, bullion, transactional currency, transactions and related data;

(2) prevent fraud; and

(3) prevent any release of account or account holder related data subject to order of a court with proper jurisdiction.

SUBCHAPTER B. ESTABLISHMENT AND ADMINISTRATION OF TRANSACTIONAL CURRENCY

Sec. 404A.0051. ESTABLISHMENT. (a) As authorized by the U.S. Const. Art. I, § 10, the comptroller shall issue specie and establish a transactional currency as determined practicable.

(b) The comptroller may preferentially contract with a private vendor having its principal place of business in Texas to establish the transactional currency or perform other duties under this chapter.

(c) In establishing the transactional currency, the comptroller shall establish a means to ensure that a person or State who holds the transactional currency may use such as legal tender in payment of debt, readily transfer or assign such transactional currency to any other person or State by electronic means.

(d) In establishing specie, the comptroller shall exclusively authorize the Texas Bullion Depository as the State's issuer and ensure that the holder of such specie may use such as legal tender in payment of debt, readily transferable to any other person or State.

Sec. 404A.0052. BULLION DEPOSITORY ACCOUNT. (a) The comptroller serving as trustee or another person appointed, by the comptroller who shall serve as trustee shall hold in trust on behalf of the transactional currency holders all specie and bullion owned or purchased for such purposes. The trustee shall maintain enough specie or bullion to provide for the redemption of all units of the transactional currency issued but not redeemed.

(b) The trustee shall establish an account in the Texas Bullion Depository to hold in trust as trustee on the behalf of the transactional currency holders all specie and bullion owned and allocated or purchased for such purposes.

Sec. 404A.0053. PURCHASE AND ISSUANCE. (a) A person or any State of the United States, may be issued their transactional currency by the comptroller upon:

(1) Making payment to the comptroller for the purpose of a purchase of specie or bullion to be represented by transactional currency together with any fee charged under Section 404A.0058; or

(2) Designating specie or bullion held on account in the Texas Bullion Depository for the purpose of being represented by

transactional currency together with payment of any fee charged under Section 404A.0058.

(b) Upon receiving payment under Sec. 404A.0053 (a)(1) or an account holder's designation and payment under Sec. 404A.0053 (a) (2), the comptroller shall:

(1) using the money received, buy specie or bullion in the number of troy ounces of precious metal equal to the number of units of the transactional currency to be issued to the purchaser under Subdivision (a); and

(2) deposit such specie or bullion into the pooled depository account for purchaser under Subdivision(a); and

(3) issue to the purchaser an account with or add to an existing transactional currency account a number of units of the transactional currency equal to the amount of specie or bullion that the purchase money received from the account holder would buy at the market price on that date as published by the Texas Bullion Depository.

Sec. 404A.0054. REDEMPTION OF TRANSACTIONAL CURRENCY FOR US DOLLARS. (a) A person who holds transactional currency may present to the comptroller any number of units of the transactional currency to redeem for US dollars.

(b) On receipt of a person's request for redemption, the comptroller shall:

(1) sell from the specie or bullion held in the pooled depository account a number of troy ounces equal to the number of units of the transactional currency being redeemed; and

(2) provide to the person an amount of US dollars equal to the amount received from the sale of specie or bullion under Subdivision (1), less a fee charged under Section 404A.0058.

Sec. 404A.0055. REDEMPTION OF TRANSACTIONAL CURRENCY FOR SPECIE OR BULLION. (a) Subject to Sec. 404A.0051 an account holder who holds the transactional currency may present to the comptroller any number of units of the transactional currency to redeem for an equal number of troy ounces of specie or bullion from the pooled depository account.

(b) On receipt of a request for redemption, the comptroller shall:

(1) withdraw the equivalent number of troy ounces of specie or bullion from the pooled depository account; and

(2) on the payment of a fee charged under Section 404A.0058, deliver the specie or bullion as requested to the requestor.

Sec. 404A.0056. VALUE OF TRANSACTIONAL

CURRENCY. (a) At the time of each transaction involving the issuance or redemption of the transactional currency, the comptroller shall determine the value of a unit of the transactional currency as published by the Texas Bullion Depository.

(b) The value of a unit of the transactional currency at the time of a transaction must be equal to the value of the appropriate fraction of a troy ounce of gold or silver, respectively at the time of that transaction as published by the Texas Bullion Depository.

Sec. 404A.0057. CERTAIN MONEY AND DEPOSITS HELD IN TRUST AND NOT SUBJECT TO LEGISLATIVE APPROPRIATION. Money received under Section 404A.0053(a), specie or bullion purchased and deposited in the pooled depository account as provided by Section 404A.0053(b)(1), and money received from the sale of specie or bullion in the pooled depository account in response to a request for redemption under Section 404A.0054 is:

(1) held by the comptroller as trustee outside the state treasury on the behalf of persons who hold the transactional currency; and

(2) not available for legislative appropriation.

Sec. 404A.0058. FEE. The comptroller may establish a fee for the issuance or redemption of the transactional currency to cover the comptroller's costs in administering this chapter and an industry standard merchant fee for use. The comptroller shall deposit the net fee proceeds after costs to the credit of an account established in the general revenue fund.

SECTION 2. This Act takes effect Janurary 1, 2024.

Use the camera on your smartphone to go download this model legislation or visit https://piratemoneybook.com/legislation.

[NOTE: Attorney Chris Byrd was instrumental in crafting this Model bill language for Texas. He was also an important part of our efforts and success with the 88th Legislature. Chris understands sound money like few attorneys in the country.]

APPENDIX B

Links to Media Coverage on the Texas Effort. Use your smartphone camera to view the following links as well as all the footnotes on the website or visit https://www.piratemoneybook.com/links.

Texas Transactional Gold Bill Glenn Beck and Brian Hughes
https://youtu.be/DmAiA-7ePlA

Texas Bill Would Allow Gold-Backed Digital Currency
https://www.conservativehq.org/post/texas-bill-would-allow-gold-backed-digital-currency

Texas Bill Would Create State-Issued Gold-Backed Digital Currency
https://schiffgold.com/key-gold-news/texas-bill-would-create-state-issued-gold-backed-digital-currency/

Texas Introduces Bill to Ban Central Bank Digital Currency (CDBC)
https://watcher.guru/news/texas-introduces-bill-to-ban-central-bank-digital-currency-cdbc

IN-DEPTH: Texas Lawmakers Consider Creating Gold-Based Digital Currency for Use by Anyone Anywhere
https://www.theepochtimes.com/in-depth-texas-lawmakers-consider-creating-gold-based-digital-currency-for-use-by-anyone-anywhere_5267493.html

Texas Transactional Gold and Silver Update and PLAN B | Ep 247
https://rumble.com/v2tqxmw-texas-transactional-gold-and-silver-update-and-plan-b-ep-247.html

Florida bans Fed digital currency; Texas bill seeks to create gold-backed digital currency
https://www.christianpost.com/news/florida-bans-fed-digital-currency-texas-eyes-gold-backed-coin.html

IN-DEPTH: Dangerous Global Shift From Dollar Driven by CCP and US Policy, Experts Say
https://www.theepochtimes.com/in-depth-dangerous-global-shift-from-dollar-driven-by-ccp-and-us-policy-experts-say_5288354.html

Digital currency built on Texas gold? Here's what's being proposed.
https://www.statesman.com/story/news/politics/state/2023/05/09/texas-senate-bill-2334-proposal-new-digital-currency-texas-gold-purchase-everyday-goods/70195299007/

Texas House Advances Gold-Backed Digital Currency Bill
https://news.bitcoin.com/texas-house-advances-gold-backed-digital-currency-bill/

Texas Proposes Gold-Backed Digital Currency
https://www.usgoldbureau.com/news/texas-proposes-gold-backed-digital-currency

APPENDIX B

Texas' gold-backed digital currency project: Law Decoded, April 3–10
https://cointelegraph.com/news/texas-gold-backed-digital-currency-project-law-decoded-april-3-10

New Gold Backed Digital Currencies - From Texas To BRICS
https://youtu.be/T6qfHDpj7n8

Texas Latest to Mull Gold-Backed Digital Currency
https://beincrypto.com/texas-mull-gold-backed-digital-currency/

State lawmakers pitch gold-backed cryptocurrency
https://gcn.com/emerging-tech/2023/04/state-lawmakers-pitch-gold-backed-cryptocurrency/384999/

The Dawn of Gold-Backed Digital Currencies: Texas and Zimbabwe Lead the Charge
https://cryptomode.com/the-dawn-of-gold-backed-digital-currencies-texas-and-zimbabwe-lead-the-charge/

Texas May Launch Its Own Gold-backed Digital Currency
https://oilprice.com/Metals/Gold/Texas-May-Launch-Its-Own-Gold-backed-Digital-Currency.html

Texas Eyes a Gold-Backed Digital Currency
https://www.nysun.com/article/texas-eyes-a-gold-backed-digital-currency

TEXAS HOUSE COMMITTEE PASSES BILL TO CREATE GOLD AND SILVER-BACKED DIGITAL CURRENCIES
https://austincountynewsonline.com/texas-house-committee-passes-bill-to-create-gold-and-silver-backed-digital-currencies/

Plan For Gold-Backed Digital Currency Emerges from Texas Legislature
https://bitcoinist.com/gold-backed-digital-currency-planned/

Is the Gold Standard Coming Back in Texas? Legislators Propose Gold-Backed Digital Currency
https://finance.yahoo.com/news/gold-standard-coming-back-texas-140340799.html

Texas House, Senate propose bills to enable a gold-backed digital currency
https://www.ledgerinsights.com/texas-digital-currency-gold-backed/

Texas lawmakers push for gold-backed state digital currency
https://coingeek.com/texas-lawmakers-push-for-gold-backed-state-digital-currency/

Next Generation Money, Part 1: Texas Re-Imagines The Dollar
https://rubino.substack.com/p/next-generation-money-part-1-texas

Lone Star State 'Will Be Silicon Valley' of Crypto: Texas Blockchain Council President
https://decrypt.co/143962/texas-will-be-silicon-valley-crypto-thanks-key-legislative-wins-texas-blockchain-council-president

Kevin Freeman Discusses A Gold Depository Being Setup in Texas That Plans To Make Gold Backed Money
https://frankspeech.com/video/kevin-freeman-discusses-gold-depository-being-setup-texas-plans-make-gold-backed-money

Episode 953: As Dollar Collapses Texas Gets Ready To Print It's Own Currency!
https://lancewallnau.com/episode-953-as-dollar-collapses-texas-gets-ready-to-print-its-own-currency/

APPENDIX B

Texas Is Paving the Way for a New Gold Standard
https://www.rogueeconomics.com/inside-wall-street/texas-is-paving-the-way-for-a-new-gold-standard/

Texas Gold-Backed Digital Currency Offers Privacy, Purchasing Power: Kevin Freeman
https://www.ntd.com/texas-gold-backed-digital-currency-offers-privacy-purchasing-power-kevin-freeman_921746.html

THE STATES' REVOLT AGAINST FED'S "MONEY" ...
https://gizadeathstar.com/2023/07/the-states-revolt-against-fed-money-facsimile-grows/

North Carolina House Passes Bill to Explore Creation of Bullion Depository Along with Gold, Silver and Crypto Reserves
https://blog.tenthamendmentcenter.com/2023/06/north-carolina-house-passes-bill-to-explore-creation-of-bullion-depository-along-with-gold-silver-and-crypto-reserves/

How US States Could Pave the Way for Currency Competition
https://mises.org/wire/how-us-states-could-pave-way-currency-competition

Could States Pave The Way For Currency Competition? | ZeroHedge
https://www.zerohedge.com/markets/could-states-pave-way-currency-competition

Economic Warfare and Financial Terrorism
https://rumble.com/v30r942-economic-warfare-and-financial-terrorism-kevin-freeman-freedom-alive-ep87.html

About the Author

KEVIN D. FREEMAN, CFA

Kevin Freeman is known as "the father of the LSV investing movement." LSV refers to investing in Liberty, Security, and Values and is the counter to hypocritical ESG (which has been hijacked to fuel corporate greed, inequality, and globalist tyranny). He is also co-founder of the National Security Investment Consultant Institute (NSIC) and Partner, EWR-Media Holdings, LLC. He is the Host of *Economic War Room with Kevin Freeman* (BlazeTV), a NY Times bestselling author, and considered one of the world's leading experts on the issues of Economic Warfare. He holds the CFA designation, and his research has been presented in critical DoD studies. He has briefed the FBI, DIA, ONA, SEC, Naval War College, HASC, Naval Postgraduate School, DARPA, IARPA, and a host of government agencies tasked with protecting America as well as members of both the House and Senate and multiple Presidential candidates.

Kevin is a citizen of the Cherokee Nation and serves as Speaker of the Cherokee Community of North Texas; a Senior Fellow at the Center for Security Policy; former Contributing Editor to *The Counter Terrorist* magazine; Trustee at Oklahoma Wesleyan University; and a member of the Advisory Board of First Liberty Institute.

His books include *Secret Weapon: How Economic Terrorism took Down the U.S. Stock Market and Why It Could Happen Again* (NY Times Bestseller), *Game Plan: How to Protect Yourself from the Coming Cyber-Economic Attack* (Amazon bestseller), and *According to Plan: The Elite's Secret Plan to Sabotage America* (Amazon bestseller).

Tell me and I forget.
Teach me and I remember.
Involve me and I learn.
—Benjamin Franklin

ACKNOWLEDGMENTS

Pirate Money was born from a powerful team effort. Hundreds of people across Texas worked to enact transactional gold and silver in the legislative session and thousands more across the nation sent emails, made phone calls, and prayed. This book would not be possible without them.

First and foremost, I hope to give glory to God who created Liberty and gave us the wonderful opportunity of life in America. Second, I wish to thank my family, my wife of a quarter-century Marnie who is more beautiful and a greater joy than when we first me, if that were possible. She has been my support, encouragement, and strength. And love to our beautiful daughters Madysen and Kieryn, both in college, who put up with their dad spending weeks of the summer holed up for research and writing. My brother Kirk and his family and sister Kelly and her family have also been terrific as have my in-laws Roger and Moe. Finally, special thanks to my dad, Kerry Freeman, who taught me the importance of Liberty and the Constitution. Love you, Dad (and Donna)!

Many of the people listed here helped in multiple areas. Even if I name them only once, they deserve appreciation for all areas and really across the board.

My partners and the team at LibertyHawk, *Economic War Room*, and the NSIC Institute have also been amazing in making the book a reality. Thank you, Russell Lake, Mike Carter, Dick U., and also Ben Parris, Jason Shane, and Van Fitzgerald. Included in this group also should be Rod Martin, former member of the PayPal Founding team who has provided intellectual heft in our many, many conversations on this topic. And Keith Green, our corporate chaplain and prayer coverer, who always has a timely word and sage advice.

Then, I owe thanks to the Texas Transactional Currency team who met practically every day that the Texas legislature was in session and at least weekly following. And many thanks to the powerful prayer warriors who joined regularly as well. I tried to get permission to name all these amazing people. Some agreed. Others declined. If I left anyone off, I apologize. Thank you, Paul Blair, Betsy Gray, Tami Barrier, Val Tharp, Chad Connelly, Marc Pitts, Gina Gleason, Rocky Christenberry, Suzanne Grishman, Anita Scott, Glenn and Jenny Story, Scott Coburn, Dave and Kris Kubal (and all the Intercessors for America), the Prayer for the Nation team, Vicki Nohrden, Marilyn R. Jackson, Garrick Pang, Scott O'Grady, Terri Hasdorff, Pauletta J. Bonner, Rick Green, Joel and Karen Starnes, Sue Evenwel, Cindy Jacobs, Audrea Decker, Tim Barton, David Barton, John M. Harrington III, Jim McClain, Gary Bennett, Anne Tate, Kent Harrington, Rick Scarborough, Angela Ruff, Dan Fisher, David Tice, Robert Douglas, Doug and Anglea Stamps, J.B. Horton, Bill Priefert, Darrel W. Johnson and Katherine A. Novikov.

Legislative wisdom came from George Pond, Matt Krause, James Dickey, Caleb Cashdollar, John Graves, Mark Dorazio, Bryan Hughes, Jason Rapert, Tan Parker, Scott and Trayce Bradford, Cindi Castilla, JoAnne Fleming, Tom Glass, and Chris Byrd. These people are amazing at understanding how to get an idea into a bill and then get it passed.

ACKNOWLEDGMENTS

We were blessed to have a great deal of coverage in the media including interviews and stories from Debbie Georgatos (*America, Can We Talk?),* Brannon Howse (*WVW* and *LindellTV*), Glenn Beck, Larry Elder, Grant Stinchfield, Alex Newman (*Epoch Times*), Frank Gaffney (*Securing America*), Craig Huey, Richard Harris, (*Truth and Liberty*) Shaun Thompson, Kevin Hogan (*NTD*), Lance Wallnau and Mercedes Sparkes (*Lance Wallnau show*), David and Stacy Whited (*Flyover Conservatives),* Sandy Rios (*Sandy Rios 24/7*), Mat Staver (*Freedom Alive*) Darlene Sanchez (*Epoch Times*), and Michael Maharrey (*10th Amendment Center*) to name a few. Special thanks to Gene Bailey and the *Flashpoint* viewers who crashed our "take action" campaign every time they had me on the show.

Let me also thank you, the reader, in advance. Please help us get the word out! This book can bring one of the greatest revolutions in monetary history. Spread the word using the QR Code. **With your help, we can send books to every legislator and state official in America and take back sound money to restore Liberty.**

Be a Pirate!

Help us get this book in the hands of as many public officials as possible. When you scan the QR code or visit www.piratemoneybook.com click on the "Pay it Forward" tab and you can purchase 10 books at a special discount. We will make sure they get delivered to the right people!

INDEX

INDEX

INDEX

INDEX